Open the Door
TO THE
TRUTH

The Truth About Getting What You Want

by

Michael Porter

*I dont believe in coincidences.
If you picked up this book. It was
meant for you.*

MPorter 2023

DORRANCE
PUBLISHING CO
EST. 1920
PITTSBURGH, PENNSYLVANIA 15238

The contents of this work, including, but not limited to, the accuracy of events, people, and places depicted; opinions expressed; permission to use previously published materials included; and any advice given or actions advocated are solely the responsibility of the author, who assumes all liability for said work and indemnifies the publisher against any claims stemming from publication of the work.

Dorrance Publishing Co
585 Alpha Drive
Suite 103
Pittsburgh, PA 15238
Visit our website at www.dorrancebookstore.com

ISBN: 978-1-6393-7078-8
eISBN: 978-1-6393-7866-1

Open the Door

TO THE

TRUTH

The Truth About Getting What You Want

by

Michael Porter

CONTENTS

THE HOOK

I can remember being about five years old and deciding that someday I was going to be a "somebody." I had no idea what that meant, but I wanted to make a difference in someone's life. I wanted to be special. I was sure from about the age of 10 that I was going to be a rockstar. The problem was that I wasn't really dedicated to that dream. It was just a dream, and no matter how many times I sang in front of the mirror, I didn't have the tools to make that dream come true.

Do you remember when adults would ask you what you wanted to be when you grew up? Did this ever happen to you? I know that it happened to me, but I don't remember what I said. I know I didn't say a rockstar. If you have never been asked this question, let me be the first. What do you want to do when you grow up? Where would you like to live? Where do you want to work? Do you want to own your own business? Who do you want to marry? What kind of car do have? How much money do you make?

Too many of us never consider these questions. We are afraid to ask these questions because we are afraid that we can never reach these dreams. It seems that we lose our dreams. When you get knocked around enough, you just stop dreaming and wanting. We lose the ability to decide what we want. I know, have you ever made a New Year's resolution, just to watch it disappear in three weeks? I love driving by the gym in January and seeing all the people who have decided to get in shape. In February, the lot is almost empty again.

What if I told you that there is a way to get what you want? Would you believe me? If you have read this far, I hope you will give me the chance to prove it. The following is a story about Jack and Diane. It's a story about how Jack and Diane learn the truth about getting what you want. The story is true, and I know all the characters personally. I will be honest, some of the characters are me and my wife at different times in our lives. I will let you try and figure out who. It's not as obvious as you might think.

All the truths in this book have been tested. I am not the only one who knows these truths. I have been lucky to see these truths work in my life as well as in the lives of so many others. Don't be fooled into thinking that they won't work for you. I see greatness in you. I hope you will read about Jack and Diane and discover how the truths of life can help you reach your dreams.

Dream big, dream vividly. Decide what you want. ✱
Mike Porter

WHY WRITE THIS BOOK?

Last week, I was talking to a gentleman I knew who had worked for his company for over five years, and he was complaining about his job. I was surprised to hear that he was unhappy since he had just gotten a promotion a few months earlier. I asked him why he was feeling so out of sorts. He said he wasn't making enough money.

"I thought you just got a promotion."

"I did, but it's more work and more hours. I think I took a pay cut."

I asked him a real simple question, "How much do you want to make?"

"I don't know," was his reply.

I was confused.

"If you don't know how much you should be making or how much you want to make, how do you know that you aren't making enough?"

He said, "That is a good point. I need to ask for a raise."

Again, I said, "How much?"

We talked for about 30 minutes, and I outlined some things he should do before asking for the raise.

Too many times, we are upset about where we are at in life, and yet we haven't really ever decided what we truly want. What our goals are.

Everything in life starts with what you want. It's easy to complain that you don't have, but that is thinking about it all wrong. It's not what your neighbor has and you don't. It's easy to look at successful people and say they got all the breaks. How can you complain about what you don't have if you don't know what you want? If you don't ever write down what you want. This leads us to where we need to start. You start with what you want.

"If you don't go after what you want, you'll never have it."

"Decide what kind of life you want, and say no to everything which isn't that."

"No wind favors him who has no destined port."
— Michel de Montaigne

We start with what we want because it helps us keep on track. Let's call it our rudder. When ships sailed the seven seas, they used the wind to power them. If we don't know what we want, we let life take us in any direction that the wind blows. If the wind blows east, we go east. Going east is great if I want to go it east, but what if going east sends you to the rocks? To me, people live their lives this way.

They seem confused and are always unhappy. They can't seem to figure out why their life hasn't turned out better. With a rudder or knowing what they want, they can steer their life in the direction they want to go. If we don't know where we want to go, we will have no idea when we are off course. Let's look at Jack and Diane.

A little ditty about Jack and Diane
Two American kids growing up in the heartland
Jack, he gonna be a football star.
Holdin' on to sixteen as long as you can
Change is coming 'round real soon.
Make us women and men.
—John Mellencamp, *American Fool*, Riva Music Ltd.

I loved this song back in the eighties; 1982, to be exact. I was 16.

"Hold on to 16 as long as you can, change is coming round real soon" speaks to me, even today. At 16, the world was my oyster. I had big dreams. I was going to be a "somebody." Nothing could or would stop me from making it big. At 16, everything seemed possible, with no probability of failure. I was safe, secure, and I now had my driver's license. Unstoppable.

"But change comes around real soon and turns us into women and men." At some point between 16 and 25, I lost something: that idealistic view that I could be anything I wanted. I think the business of life got in the way. Minor failures, laziness, and the lack of understanding of what it took to be successful stopped me in my tracks. At 25, something clicked, and I got put back on the right track. The more I think about it though, I met the woman of my dreams, and she put me back on track.

First Truth
Science has shown that the right partner can make life so much better. This may seem like an obvious truth. That's the beauty; truth is truth regardless if you believe it or you don't. Having the right partner in life makes it easier to reach for what you want. You want someone who believes in you more than you believe in yourself. You want someone who will kick you in the butt. You want someone who sees all your potential. If you find that person, don't ever let them go; they are greater than gold. (Thank you for being that for me, Pea.)

Success is a journey, and I believe your journey could be more successful if you follow the simple truths. For the next couple of hours follow Jack and Diane's journey. Please note these are made up characters, and by no means are a representation of Jack and Diane that John Mellencamp sings about.

Jack and Diane have been married for two years. They live on the bottom floor of a 10-year-old apartment complex. Rent has gone up every year that they have lived there. The neighbors on the floor above them keep them up most nights. The neighbors are night owls, and it makes for a difficult living situation. ✴

THE MEETING

One day early in his shift, Jack was called into the boss's office. This was unusual. Jack had never been called to the boss's office before; he wondered what he did wrong. The boss had Jack sit down and he sat right next to him.

"Jack, I've been watching you for a while, and I see great things in you. I want to know, what do you want?"

"Excuse me?" A look of confusion crossed Jack's face. He shuddered for a minute.

"I don't want anything. I'm a simple man, Diane and I are happy and content."

The boss pressed for more information.

"Jack, life shouldn't be about settling for fine. God does not intend for us just to survive. He wants us to thrive. He wants us to be the light. We are born to shine. No one hides a light under a bowl. Jack, I want you to thrive! This is very important. I want you to go home and talk with your wife and discuss what you want this year. I want to help you get there."

"So let me get this straight. You want to know what I want? Can I have some context?"

The boss laughed.

"It's pretty straight forward. I want to know what you want. For your family, for your career, for your life."

Jack squinted his eyes. He was trying to decide if the boss was teasing him. His mind started to race; he could hear that voice in his head. It was saying, *This is a trap. Be very careful.*

What did he want? He hadn't really thought about what he wanted. At least not seriously. He wanted that Range Rover that he saw yesterday. He wouldn't mind a 60-inch TV with surround sound. A vacation to Maui would be nice.

So what? These were really only pipe dreams.

"I will go home and talk with Diane, but I don't really see how this will help."

The boss nodded his head.

"I know. I guess you are just going to have to trust me. I will talk with you tomorrow."

With that Jack left the boss's office. As he walked back to his office, all he could think was, *That was the weirdest meeting that he had ever had…* How was he going to talk with Diane about this?

That night Jack went home and complained to Diane, "My boss was being weird today."

"Hmmm? I thought you liked your boss," said Diane.

"I do. But he wants to know what I want, what we want."

Diane was confused.

"What do you mean he wants to know what you want?"

"That's the funny thing. I'm not sure. He told me that we are meant to thrive, and he wants to help us get what we want."

"Why would he want us to tell him what we want?" Diane was as concerned that Jack's boss was getting a little too personal. What business was it of his?

"He says that knowing what you want is the only way you can get it. He said, 'Let's test the theory.' He wants us to come up with one thing that we want for the upcoming year. He said that he could show us how to get there."

For the next few minutes, Jack and Diane just looked at each other. They had never heard anything so outlandish in their whole lives.

"This is crazy," said Diane. "Just deciding what we want would help us attain it?"

Just then, the neighbors above them came home and started playing their stereo extremely loud. Both Jack and Diane's eyes lit up. In unison, they both said, "A house!"

Both Jack and Diane were certain that this was just a dream. Even though Jack and Diane both thought this was a long shot, they decided that Jack should take this "want" back to his boss and see what happened.

They agreed, buying a home is exactly what they needed. With that agreement, they got ready for bed, and it was obvious that both Jack and Diane where in deep thought about the idea. They kissed and drifted off to sleep, thinking about the possibilities.

The next morning, Jack woke up to, worry swirling around his head. *A house in this market, who are we kidding?* They could barely afford the apartment. How were they going to be able to get a house? *We are just setting ourselves up for failure and disappointment.*

Before Jack left for work, he told Diane he wasn't sure that they should share wanting a house.

"Maybe this is too big of a want. It's not like the boss is going to buy us a home. This is just too much."

Diane said, "Jack do you trust your boss?" Jack thought for a moment and nodded yes. "Then let's test his theory." ✦

QUESTIONS

As soon as Jack got into work, he went straight to his boss's office. The boss was on the phone talking with someone and held up a finger for him to wait a minute and sit down. As Jack walked in, he noticed a board on his wall. He'd never paid attention to it before, and it was odd that he saw it now. It was a collage of a bunch of different cut-out pictures. They look like pictures out of a magazine, they weren't in any particular order, and they looked like a third grader had cut them out and glued them to the board. Jack started to study the collage, and things seemed to make sense. He still wasn't sure why, but they looked familiar. He just couldn't put his finger on it.

"Jack, did you talk with Diane?"

"Yes, Diane and I spoke, and we don't see how deciding what we want will make any difference. I've wanted lots of things in life, and to be honest with you, they never really panned out. You know you get hit in the teeth enough times. You just stop wanting anything."

The boss nodded his head and said, "I understand. I've been there. I would dream of a nice car, a lovely house, family, friends, but I never thought about what it would look like, how it would smell, how vivid it would be. My dreams were just whispers in the night. Like a fleeting thought and then I would go on with my day.

"See, I never gave it a second thought, and since I didn't give it a second thought, I wouldn't always make the right decisions to go after what I wanted. When you decide what you want, when you write it down and see every piece of it, you start the engine of getting what you want. You begin to think about the decisions that you need to make to get there. When we don't truly consider what we want, we are like a rudderless ship. We just go wherever the wind blows us. This is not a way to live life. It's quite simple when you think about it. How good is a ship if we can't make it go where we want?

"Let's take it even a step further; let's say you have a boat. Don't you decide where you want to go? Of course, you do. No one pulls their boat to the forest with the hope that there will be a lake to put the boat in. And finally, we would never take a boat into the lake if we had no way to steer it. This is why we need to figure out what we want. This does not mean that we will always get what we want, but it gives us a starting point. A point to aim for. It provides a way to determine if our choices are taking us closer or farther away from where we want to be. Do you understand?"

"Okay, I think I understand, but this seems way too simple to work."

"You are right," said the boss. "The problem with success and getting what you want, is that it is simple. Don't get me wrong; it still takes a lot of work, but like most things in life, we look past the simple and try to find the hard things to make our lives worthwhile. If we embrace the simple things and have discipline, we could make our lives and the world a better place."

"Okay, I'm not sure I understand what you mean by 'do the simple things.'" Jack was lost. Do the simple things? That made no sense. All the successful people he knew seemed to have mastered the highest mountains. I mean, they were lucky; or they came from a great, wealthy family; or they were very athletic. None of these people had real struggles. They took giant leaps in life. That's why they got what they wanted. Jack suddenly realized that his boss had stopped talking and was just studying him. How long had the boss stopped talking?

I wasn't talking out loud, was I? Why is he looking at me like that?

A slight smile was on the boss's face now, like he knew what Jack was thinking.

"Jack, I know all of this seems way too easy to work. I assure you that going after what you want is going to take work and sacrifice. Everything in life comes at a cost. It's all about choice, and we will talk about that later."

"Success is simple. It's easy to do the things that need to be done. The problem is, it's even more comfortable not to do them."

Jack said, "That kind of makes sense, but can we go back to knowing what you want first? Are you saying if I know what I want, I will just get it by knowing? Wouldn't that mean I could have everything I ever wanted? Do you have all the things that you decided you wanted? If it's that easy, why doesn't everyone do it?"

"These are great questions, Jack. Let's take each question separately. I will try to answer them, so they make sense."

Now the boss was smiling. Jack didn't know it then, but the boss was glad that Jack had had all these questions. It meant that Jack was curious, and curious people made things happen. And this was precisely what he wanted for Jack and Diane.

Question #1: Will I get everything I want by just knowing what I want?

"If this is true, I'm starting a Christmas list early this year," said Jack.

"Jack that is a perfect analogy for how knowing what you want.. Do you remember as a kid getting the Sears catalog?"

Jack's face squinted up like he ate a lemon.

"What is the Sears catalog?"

The boss laughed out loud and almost spat out his coffee all over his desk.

"I'm sorry, Jack, I forgot you are a bit younger than I am. When I was a kid, about two months before Christmas, the department store Sears would mail out this 300-page color catalog with pictures and descriptions of all the things it sold. As a kid, we always knew that Christmas was right around the corner when we saw that catalog. Almost every kid in America loved that catalog because we could see all the top toys that would be available that year.

"There was page after page after page of different toys. There was boring stuff, like school clothes and adult stuff, but kids like me never looked at them. My sister and I would take turns looking and dreaming about what we would get. We each would take a colored pen and circle all the things we wanted for Christmas. Some years, we may each have had up to 100 items that we wanted for Christmas. We would go through that catalog several times over. Each time, we would dream of how great it would be if we had each toy.

"Did we get everything we circle in the catalog? Of course not, our parents weren't wealthy, and even if they were, that's not how life works. Usually, around December 1, our parents would ask us to put a star next to the top 10 gifts we wanted. And usually, we would get five or six of the things that we starred, depending on the budget that year.

"Would we be disappointed that we didn't get all the hundred presents? Yes, maybe sometimes but it was a great lesson in life. Everything comes at a cost. Sometimes I would want an expensive toy, which meant I would get fewer toys. Knowing this helped me make a decision. I knew that I would have to give up nine small toys to get one expensive toy. The question becomes, would I have gotten the toy that I wanted if I hadn't circled it in the first place? Why sure, I would have gotten presents, and maybe just by luck, I would've gotten one of the things that I wanted. But that would be leaving it to chance.

"Why would I leave it to chance? Is it hard to circle items in a catalog? No, it's easy. My parents had reinforced this discipline by rewarding us with what we wanted. We didn't get everything and again this trained us to ask for what we really wanted.

"Life is just like picking what you want from a Sears catalog. First, you choose everything that you would like, and then you narrow it down. In life, we narrow it down because there are only so many hours in a day. We narrow it down because some things are just more important for us and to us. By rule, I like to pick items every year that coincides with my family, health, finances, fun and spirituality."

Jack started to understand.

Question #2: Can I have whatever I want?

"In the process of figuring out what we want, we need to write it down. During the process of figuring out what we want, sometimes we realize what we want isn't right for us at this time."

Jack was confused.

"I'm not sure I get it. What you mean it might not be the right time?"

"By figuring out what you want, you can better decide if what you are working for is the best thing for you at this time. Let me give you an example: if you came back to me, and you and Diane had said that you wanted a fancy sports car. Don't get me wrong; there is nothing wrong with a sports car. In fact, there is nothing that says you can't work towards the sports car goal. When you start putting the plan into action, you may begin to realize that the cost is too high for where you are in life right now."

Jack interrupted and said, "Wait a minute, so I'm only supposed to want things I can afford?"

"Great question, Jack. That is not what I mean. What I mean is that the reward may cost you more than you're willing to give at this time. If the sports car is all you want, you can have it. You may also decide that the sports car can be one of the things you want instead of the only thing you want.

"You are a young man with a wife, and I have heard you talk about starting a family. It may be that it's not the right time to get a sports car. And by getting the sports car, it may make the other wants suffer. That's why it's so important to decide what you want for your family, for your salary, your home, your wife, and your investments. Just remember, everything comes at a cost. And I don't mean just money. I mean time, energy, commitment, and love. The beauty of deciding what you want allows you to say no to the things you don't want."

Knowing what you do want allows you to say no to things you don't want.

"Does that make sense?"

Jack thought for a moment.

"I guess what you're saying is, when I pick things I want, it doesn't necessarily mean I'll get everything, but it starts me off on the right track to decide what is most important to me in my life. Really, what you're saying is, without knowing what I want, my odds of getting them are up to chance. By choosing what I want even though I might not get everything on my list, I will move closer to some of those things. The things I don't get won't be because of chance, but because I chose not to go after them. Those items on my list just were not as is vital to me."

"Exactly! I could not have said it better myself," said the boss.

Question #3: Why doesn't everyone do it?

"The last question is tough to answer. The easy answer is that people just don't know. It just seems too easy. We have been convinced that to have what we want takes an incredible amount of luck. We may decide that we don't deserve what we want. Maybe we wanted things just to be disappointed by the results. We have this misconception if we don't get what we want on the first try, then it wasn't meant to be.

"Some people see failure as a result or a statement about their future. Successful people aren't the ones that get it right the first time. They relish the journey. They know anything worthwhile takes faith, hard work, and a lot of falling flat on their face. Knowing what you want allows you to pick yourself up and keep going. This first truth will enable us not to stop and look at each failure as a defect but as a stepping stone to success."

The first truth will enable us to look at failure not as a defect,
but as a stepping stone to success.

Jack wondered to himself if this could possibly be true.

"The deeper you look at this truth, the more you'll see that getting what you want is never a giant leap. It's small steps every day. We get so caught up in trying to get what we want in a single bound. That thought can defeat us before we even start. The leap can seem like jumping the Grand Canyon. But as you put this truth to the test, what you will find is that the real reward isn't getting what you want, but learning how to get there. The lessons that we learn on the journey far outweigh the actual goal. You asked if it's so easy, why don't more people do it? The reason is most people don't test this first truth. All they see is the Grand Canyon. They never look for the path that will take them through the canyon; instead, they look right over the canyon. People let their minds play tricks on them and tell them that they could never make it, even if they do see the path.

"Getting what we want takes time and effort. I think the final reason is the energy it takes to start. Chemists call this 'active energy.' It is the minimum amount of energy required to initiate a chemical reaction. Psychologists have picked up this term to describe the motivation needed to begin a task. This means that it takes a lot of mind power to start."

Sean Anchor in his book *Happiness Advantage* says that the brain is lazy. It uses the easiest route to accomplish things. The brain is always looking for ways to conserve energy.

"When you start thinking about what you want, the brain is in complete agreement and tells you, 'Let's do it.' But if all you do is have a fleeting thought about what you want, the brain starts to calculate how much energy it will take to get there. This is where your brain convinces you that it takes way too much energy to get it done. Successful people realize this rule, and they do things to get past this activating energy problem. They start small by first deciding what they want, then they write it down, and then they envision precisely how it will be once they get there. Once they know what they want, they put what they want in front of them every day, but we'll go over that later.

"Tonight, please go back home and talk with Diane about the things we have discussed. Tonight, I want you to hone in on the one thing that you have picked. Write it down. I mean everything, all the details: what it is, what color it is, where it is, and how it makes you feel. Go dream and imagine like there are no limits on what it would look like. I also want you and Diane to consider the other aspects of your life. What else do you want to want? But first, let's focus on this one thing. What would I want if there was no concern for getting it? No worries about money, time, and there is no chance of failure. Make a list of these things, and we will discuss them next week."

★ ★ ★ **TRUTH** ★ ★ ★

You need to know what you want, so you don't leave it to chance.
Think big. No limits. Write it down. Do it now! ★

THE SECRET

At this point, Jack's head was swimming. He was excited and scared all the same time. He kept thinking this may be one of the greatest secrets he had ever learned. Why did his boss keep saying it wasn't a secret? He had never heard this before.

The boss knew what Jack was thinking and said, "Let me leave you with these two thoughts:

"First thought, this is no secret. The reason you don't know about this first great truth is you stopped listening. You stopped believing you can have what you want. And you're not the only one. For some reason, we have let disappointment and failure teach us that we are not destined for greatness. We started to believe that failure was an endpoint of our journey. We begin to think that risk leads to failure and disappointment. We believe that winning is the best reward and that if we participate, we should get a trophy.

"Unfortunately, this is not how life works. We don't always get a medal. Life isn't about just showing up. However, that is a good start. But then you have to 'do.' We gain so much from our failures, especially if you look at them correctly. When we look at failure as a learning opportunity. We change the meaning entirely. I like to call it 'failing forward.' I choose to look at what I did, what choices I made, and what I've learned. I am continually asking myself, 'What did I learn from this?' This changes the whole concept of failing and lets me look at life in a completely different way."

"Second thought, what I'm asking you to do next week. It's something that less than 10 percent of people will ever do. I want you to search for the truth. I want you to read about great people; I want you to study how others got what they wanted. I want you to read for at least 30 minutes a day. Read about sales, finance, how to be a better husband and father, leadership, joy, happiness, and God. I want you to be curious about what makes one person a success and another person a failure. My journey started when I wanted have a better garden. I want you to imagine that you are a farmer. What do farmers do in the winter?"

Jack looked confused.

"I'm not sure."

"That's okay. In this day and age where food just shows up at the grocery store, we hardly ever put any thought into the process. As you probably know, I am not a farmer, and I failed miserably at my small garden. Every year, I seem to yield a minimal crop. Some items would overgrow and other things would not grow at all. I love the process, though. You know, reaping what you sow.

"The problem was, I didn't put any thought into my garden. It was usually planted on a whim. I would be at Home Depot or Lowe's, and I would see plants on sale, and I would think, *Yeah, let's plant a garden...*

"I would take the plants home, dig a hole, put the plants in the ground, and wait until summer to pick the fruit. Isn't this a great metaphor for life? We do things on a whim, hoping and praying for the fruit to come, and then we are disappointed when our yield is small or doesn't produce any fruit at all. This was my problem. I was leaving out valuable steps to make my garden produce a high volume of fruits and vegetables.

"After many years of mildly successful vegetable gardening, I happened to be sitting next to a man at our church, and he was an actual successful farmer. After church, I had an opportunity to talk with him, and I asked him if he had a minute to talk about farming because I was having issues with my garden."

✦ ✦ ✦ TRUTH ✦ ✦ ✦
Ask, and it shall be given to you, seek and ye shall find,
knock and it shall be opened unto you:
for everyone that asks receives; and he that seeks finds;
and to him that knocks it shall be opened.
—Matthew 7:7-8

When we don't know something, or even if we kind of know something, it is okay to ask an expert or someone with a greater knowledge on how to do something. Don't let fear get in your way. My experience is that 90 percent of people are more than happy to share their expertise, specifically when you have a real interest. Most people never ask because they are afraid of rejection. Don't let that get in your way. Even if someone denies you, don't take it personally. There are several reasons why someone will say no. I've always decided if a person is unwilling or unable to share with me, it's just meant there's someone better for me to talk to.

There is a time for everything, in a season for every activity under heaven.
— Ecclesiastes

The boss said, "I think this is all the time we have for today. You have your assignment. I hope you will give it an honest effort, and we will talk next week about my time with the farmer."

Jack was happy that the meeting was over. Not that the meeting was terrible, but he had a lot to think about and share with Diane.

That evening, Jack was contemplating all that the boss had shared with him. Was he living his life like a gardener who does things on a whim?

Diane came home from work and saw Jack sitting in his chair. He called it his "thinking chair." Diane thought it should be called his "escape chair." Jack didn't even look up when she entered the apartment. The music was blaring from the neighbors upstairs.

"It looks like the neighbors have started early this evening." Jack didn't even blink. Was he okay? "Jack, are you alive?"

Jack look startled.

"When did you get home?"

Diane laughed, "I've been home for a couple minutes. Where were you? You look deep in thought."

Jack shook his head.

"I was thinking about being a farmer."

"A farmer? What happened at your meeting? I don't understand. I don't want to be a farmer's wife. That sounds like a lot of work."

Now Jack laughed.

"No, I don't want to be a farmer. The boss talked to me about the first truth."

"What is the first truth?" Diane started to relax. She was concerned that Jack had had a stroke.

"The first truth is knowing what you want. It's hard to explain. No, I'm sorry; it's not hard to explain. It makes perfect sense. I think. I'm still trying to wrap my head around it. The boss said that we live our lives like an undisciplined gardener."

"Undisciplined gardener? Well, that shows how much he knows us. We haven't ever planted a garden in our lives."

Jack shook his head.

"That's not what I mean. Imagine that we went shopping and saw some plants and decided to plant a garden. What would we do?"

Diane was confused, but she decided she would play along.

"Okay, we would buy the plants that we want and go put them in the ground. Tada—a garden.

"You're correct. Most people don't even decide to start a garden, and they do it on a whim."

"What you mean?"

"The reality of it is we have never thought about starting a garden because we didn't have a place to plant it. But if we did, most likely, we would come across the idea while we were at, let's say, Home Depot. We would see tomato plants on sale, and maybe we would decide at that moment that we would like to have fresh tomatoes. Perhaps we would get excited about the possibilities of a garden. The problem is that we have done it in the wrong order."

"Why is that the wrong order? Aren't we supposed to go after what we want?"

Jack pondered that for a moment.

"I think that's a half-truth. Yes, we should go after what we want. But you need to start with deciding what you want first and then go after it. If you go after things on a whim, there is a possibility that you will not follow through with what you really want. The problem is getting what you want takes work. If we bought the plants, but we only kind of want a garden, we will not get the fruits of our labor. I'm not saying that I understand entirely. The boss wants us to talk about the things we want. It's the rudder that steers the ship."

Diane smiled. She decided that she needed to know more before she was going to take this idea seriously. She would humor Jack and help come up with something that she wanted, but this would be a waste of time.

"Let's sleep on it, and we can talk more about it tomorrow. Now get up and help me make dinner."

Jack smiled and agreed. For the first time in a long time, he felt a smidge of hope. ✶

THE FARMER

The next week flew by. Jack and Diane discussed lots of things that they wanted. They still hadn't put them down on paper, but they knew that Jack would talk with the boss and find out how important that was to this whole "truth" thing.

The time had finally come to meet with the boss again. Jack knocked on the door, and the boss waved him in. Jack sat down and noticed the collage again. He wanted to make sure to ask the boss about the group of pictures.

"So how did the discussion go with your wife? Did you think more about what we talked about?"

Jack shifted in his seat and said, "Yes, Diane and I spoke, and we came up with a few more items that we want."

"Excellent, I can't wait for you to tell me more."

Jack squirmed a little.

"I was hoping you could tell me more about your meeting with the farmer. I felt that your story with the farmer might answer some more of the questions I have about this 'truth' thing."

"That is very wise, Jack. I will share more about the farmer. Let's see…I left off where I had asked the farmer for some tricks to make my garden grow."

Jack nodded in agreement.

"And I was at church, that's right. Oh yeah, the farmer laughed and said, 'Son, I'd be happy to talk with you. I'm up very early and would love to have coffee with you tomorrow morning at 6:00 a.m.'

"The farmer could tell that I was a little concerned about that time of the morning. He said, 'We farmers do not have banker's jobs; our jobs are never 8:00-5:00, and most successful people I know are early risers.'

"Even though I had trepidation about meeting him at 6:00 in the morning, I agreed and made plans to meet him."

⋆ ⋆ ⋆ TRUTH ⋆ ⋆ ⋆
Waking up one hour earlier a day will add 15 days in the year.

"As I drove home, I wondered if my garden was worth getting up for so early. It was a decision I have never regretted. The farmer became a mentor to me and taught me things that have helped me build this business and many more. I am hoping I'll be able to mentor you in the same way.

"Getting up at 5:00 a.m. was going to be difficult. I usually got up around 7:00 and drove myself to work and showed up around 8:00-ish. Never really late, but not early either. That evening, I set my alarm for 5:00 a.m., and I hit the snooze button twice. I knew that it would take me about 15 minutes to get out to his place, and I figured it would only take me a few minutes to get ready. Unfortunately, it took me 30 minutes to prepare because the dog got sick on the floor, and I had to clean the mess up. I guess I didn't know where I was going, and I got a little lost, so instead of showing up at 6:00 a.m., it was almost 6:30 by the time I pulled into his driveway.

"When I finally arrived. The farmer was walking out of his house and greeted me with a smile. 'I didn't think you were coming,' he said.

"I explained to him all that had happened, and I was sorry that I was late. The farmer nodded and said that he understood and things happen. But he had to get to his day job. He would be happy to reschedule, but his time was very precious, and it should be for me, too. He gave me a hearty handshake and said, 'Let's do it again tomorrow.'

"Now mind you, I just wanted to talk to him about my garden and how to yield more vegetables. I said, 'Okay,' but I was a little put-off. I mean, what was so important that he couldn't answer just a few questions? This turned out to be a complete waste of time. Here I had gotten up early and drove all this way, and still, I wasn't able to talk about my garden.

"That night when I got home, my wife asked me how my meeting went with the farmer. I told her that I was about 20 minutes late, and that he said he had important things to do and that he could not meet with me again until tomorrow. She asked me how I felt about what he had said. I told her that I was kind of upset. I mean, I got up early and drove all that way, and he didn't have the time for me. 'I think he might not be the right guy to talk to about my garden. I mean, it wasn't my fault. I got up early. How was I supposed to know that there would be traffic and the dog would get sick? Maybe I will call him and cancel. I am not sure I care how to grow our garden.'

"For the next couple of hours, I contemplated calling the farmer and canceling the appointment. The more I thought about it, a feeling just came over me. The feeling just kept saying, *You have to make this appointment.* I had heard once that you have to learn from your mistakes. So, did I make a mistake? Was there something I could've done differently? Did I like the outcome? I didn't get the result that I desired, so what could I do differently?

⋆ ⋆ ⋆ TRUTH ⋆ ⋆ ⋆

When things don't go your way, don't make excuses. We have the power to make our lives better. It is our decisions that create our lives. Make bad decision, your life will not turn out the way you want; make good decision and you will end up in a better place.

It is small decision's made every day that makes all the difference. Own your decisions. You have the power.

"After further thought on the matter. I decided, that it was my fault that I didn't get the time with the farmer that I wanted. I did not make it a priority. I had made a poor decision. I would not do it again.

"I made a plan. I put out my clothes before I went to bed. I set my alarm for 4:30 a.m. I decided to get to bed an hour early, and it was amazing how smooth my morning went on try number two. Having my clothes all picked out made it much easier to get up and cut my time of getting ready. I read somewhere that Mark Zuckerberg wears the same clothes every day, so it gives him one less thing to think about it the morning. I am not suggesting that you do this, but it is an interesting concept. I was amazed how much time I saved by deciding on what I would wear the night before.

"I was out of the house before five and made it to the farmer's home with almost 15 minutes to spare. It gave me a couple of minutes to prepare for my meeting. Knowing how important time was to the farmer, I wanted to make sure that I didn't waste it."

✴ ✴ ✴ TRUTH ✴ ✴ ✴

Time is important. You show respect to others when you are on time. Make a decision today to always be 15 early. This 15-minute window allows for the unforeseen events that sometimes happen. Time is essential, so don't waste it. Treat time like gold.

Evaluate. Do all you can do to make it count. Use your evenings to help set up your day. Plan your day before you go to bed.

It may not always work out the way you plan, but it gives your mind something to focus on while you sleep. It's amazing how much your subconscious can do for you when you sleep.

Jack's Journal

—Make the best use of your time
—Time is important be early
—Prep the day before
—Have a plan ✱

LESSON ON TIME

"After a couple of minutes of sitting in my car. the farmer came out with a mug of steaming hot coffee for me. He was smiling and said he would 'make me a farmer yet.' I wasn't sure if that's what I wanted, but I was happy that we would get a chance to talk.

"We went into his house with the wonderful smell of bacon and cooked eggs in the air. He asked me if I had eaten breakfast yet. I said, 'No, I don't usually have time for breakfast.'

"The farmer smiled and asked, 'Why?'

"'I don't usually have time in the morning because I'm usually running late.'

"The farmer laughed and said, 'Like yesterday?' I shrugged, feeling pretty embarrassed, and he put me at ease. 'Those things happen. That's why it's so important to give yourself extra time to get things done. We never know what life will throw at us if we are not prepared. By giving ourselves the extra time, we usually can take care of those unexpected emergencies that may come up. What did you do differently this time?'"

"I told him about putting my clothes out, waking up earlier, and leaving early.

"'What was your outcome?'

"I looked at him funny. 'Is that a trick question?'

"The farmer laughed out loud, like I had told him the funniest joke he'd ever heard.

"'No, it is not a trick question. It is just, so many times in life we don't consider why things ended up the way they do. We never think about what we could have changed. What could we do different so that it doesn't happen again? If we make the change, is there a better result? Will we get the desired results? If we do, can we repeat it? Is the reward worth the change?'

"'You know I never thought about it before, what I can say? I am happy that I got here on time and that I have a chance to eat a great breakfast.' The farmer seemed pleased and patted me on the back and walked me to the table, and had me take a seat.

"Jack, I know this may seem like a long story, but stay with me. You see, I have had many meetings with the farmer, and based on many of the truths that he shared, I have built a very successful business and life. Those truths I still practice today."

The story enthralled Jack. He had always thought that the boss had been born successful, and he was shocked to hear that it wasn't true. He had always believed that the boss was well educated, and he always knew what he wanted to do and be. And that it came easy to him. He was intrigued that this man actually had trials, failures and not everything had come easy.

⋆ ⋆ ⋆ TRUTH ⋆ ⋆ ⋆

Ninety percent of really successful people have had many failures in their life. They separate themselves from the crowd by being learners and by taking risks. They take time every evening to measure their success to measure their failures. They decide what went well and what they have learned.

Journal your thoughts every night. Break down what happened, even when you don't have the answer. W rite down the questions that you have so you can put them in your subconscious. When you sleep, your mind will go to work and help you with the answers.

The boss took a deep breath and continued to tell his story.

"During breakfast, the farmer asked me about my life. Like you, I was unsure about what I wanted, where I wanted to go, and what my real dreams were. After each question, the farmer smiled and nodded, like he understood where I was at in my life.

"'Why are you interested in farming?' he asked.

"Now I laughed, 'I don't mean any offense, but I'm not interested in farming. I want to know if you can give me any hints about growing my garden. It seems to me that it makes sense to go to the expert. You have a huge farm, and I've had the opportunity to see and taste your harvest. I guess you are the expert, and I'm tired of struggling with my small yield, and I want to get better at it.'"

⋆ ⋆ ⋆ TRUTH ⋆ ⋆ ⋆

Seek the answers from people who have done it before. Wise people understand that we all start out as novices. The quickest way to learn is to seek out those who have done it before us. They don't even have to be alive. Many of the most extraordinary people of our time have written or have had books written about them. Never underestimate the wisdom of people from the past. Wisdom is always wisdom; never stop learning.

"The farmer again gave me his warm smile.

"'Now we're talking. I can help you with your garden, and you will be amazed at how much it will also help you in your life. If you can make the correlation between farming and success in life, this will be a very productive encounter. To be a good farmer, you need to know what season you are in. Do you know what I mean?'

"'Are you talking about the seasons of the year?'

"'Exactly! We have four seasons in a year winter, spring, summer, and fall. The seasons are critical to a farmer. The seasons are also crucial for your personal growth. The Bible says there is a time for everything. It's important to know what season you are in.'

"'They make perfect sense to me. I know that I wouldn't start planting in the winter.' The farmer nodded in agreement.

"'That is correct. Each season brings about different responsibilities. Knowing what season you're in is the start to being a successful farmer. Unfortunately, not enough people realize it's also what makes people successful. Now don't get me wrong, there are plenty of people who know about the seasons, and they still do nothing about it. Every season requires action. Knowledge without action is pointless. The point that I'm making,' said the farmer, 'is I will share my wisdom, but it is up to you to put it into action. If you do not choose to put it into action, our time together will be wasted.'

"He then became very quiet. He left me to ponder what he had said, and we had run out of time.

"'I know that you want more. Would you be willing to meet me in three days?'

"I said, 'Yes,' and I spent the next two days pondering the conversation. Much of what was said seemed to be just out of my reach of understanding. The seasons, what did they mean? I had read the Scriptures about there being a time for everything. I looked it up to see if I could decipher what the farmer was describing."

Jacks Journal
−Knowledge is not enough. You need action
−Always continue learning
−There is a time for everything
−Measure your failure
what worked
what didn't
How do I replicate my success *

WINTER TIME

There is a time for everything and a season for every activity under the heavens.
—Ecclesiastes 3:1

He has made everything beautiful in its time.
—Ecclesiastes 3:11

"I must've read those scriptures 100 times, and I'm not sure that I completely understood their meaning, but I felt like the farmer would help me understand. I waited with anticipation, and I could hardly go to sleep the night before our next meeting. I again put my clothes out the night before and set my alarm for 4:30 a.m.

"That morning I woke up right when my alarm went off, and I hopped out of bed. After being late for the first appointment, I started to change my morning habit. For three days in a row, I got up early and got prepared for my day. It was amazing how much better I felt by not feeling rushed. Again, I was at the farmer's house 15 minutes early, and I sat in my car preparing. I had started reading John Maxwell's book the *15 Invaluable Laws of Growth*[1]. In it, he says that he mentored a guy named Courtney McBeth," the boss said to John.

"'Here's what I asked. Here's what you shared. Here's what I did. Now can I ask more questions?' I decided this would be my mantra whenever I was with the farmer.

"On cue, the farmer came out of his house about five minutes before we were scheduled to meet again with a mug of hot coffee. He looked like he was glowing from the porch light. I got out of my car and walked into his home. He asked me if I would like breakfast. I told him no; with the new schedule, I had had time to eat before I got there. He seemed pleased, but I wasn't sure since I was still trying to figure him out. He took a big sip from his mug.

"'Where should we begin? What questions do you have for me about farming or, in a smaller sense planting your garden?'

"Suddenly, I became a little nervous. Was I here to waste this man's time talking about my simple garden? I'm sure I looked like a deer in headlights. I stammered a little and answered, 'Yes. I wanted to know if there were any secrets to planting a garden.'

"With a hearty laugh, the farmer said, 'There are no secrets. The biggest secret in life is that there are no secrets. Just things we haven't decided to notice. It's really about truths that we just haven't opened our minds to see. Okay, let me ask you a couple of questions. How big a garden do you plan on having? Do you want fruit or vegetables? What kind of fruit? What kind of vegetables? Do you want herbs?

How much space do you have? What type of soil? And finally, how much time do you want to spend on this garden?'

"I was about to answer when, he said, 'This is what we do in the winter. We decide what we are going to plant in the spring. We consider what we grew last year and then we decide if we want the same crop again. Sometimes, it doesn't make sense to plant the same crop because the ground may be tired. Winter is the time for dreaming and deciding what we want to grow. Dream about the yield that we are anticipating. We envision what it will look like, smell like, and how it will feel and taste. We visualize the harvest. In some ways, the wintertime is the most fun part of the year because we get to dream. So, we start with what we want. Think big! Dream like nothing can hold you back from the harvest you want.'"

∗ ∗ ∗ TRUTH ∗ ∗ ∗
You must know what you want before you get to go where you want to go.

"The farmer stopped cold when he saw my face. It was a cross look between, 'Hey, what kind of rube do you think I am?' and 'This guy has eaten too many of his own turnips.' The farmer sat back in his chair, rubbed his chin, and smiled.

"'So you are having a difficult time believing this is where you start?' Without letting me answer, he continued, 'We are almost out of time. I know you came here to talk about your garden. I hope that you'll take the advice about your garden and apply it to your life. All gardeners start with good soil: your brain, your beliefs, how you see yourself, and how you see opportunity. Many people don't realize that everyone has rich soil, but nothing grows without a seed. You have to plant the right seeds in your soil to have a great garden. The seeds in your life are your dreams and your wants. But you must be careful. Because your soil is so rich, anything can grow in it. If we plant nothing and let the soil set, it becomes fertile ground for an infestation of weeds. These weeds will flower and look nice from afar, but they only produce more weeds. People can even become comfortable with their weeds.'

"'The weeds are our thoughts and beliefs that have no truth or partial truths or half-truths. These half-truths can destroy our soil and make it very hard to plant any seeds of success. The half-truths can be something that someone told us, or most likely, it is the things we say to ourselves that we keep plowing into the ground. We say things like, *I'm so stupid.* Or *I'm a simple person, and I don't want anything.* These are half-truths. Although it may be true that you have made mistakes, who hasn't? If you aren't failing and making mistakes, you aren't testing the truths of success. Failure is only a definition for people who stop and let it define them. When we let failures, big or small, define us, we let weeds take hold of our soil. Remember, weeds are nasty, and they can take over our garden if we ignore them and do not pull them before their root system flourishes.'

"'One weed can lead to many weeds in a very short time. Our brains listen to what we tell it. It doesn't know you are stupid. It only knows what you tell it.

Whatever you plant in the soil, it will grow and multiply. When you say things like *I'm so stupid*, your brain goes, *I didn't know that about you, but I don't want you to be a liar, so I will find all the things you do wrong and make sure you notice them. All of them.* Every time you see the mistake or the failure and say *I'm so stupid*, weeds grow more robust and create a root system in your garden. This system of weeds will multiply very fast. When we let the weeds take hold, all we can see is weeds, and it becomes harder and harder to see any possibility for the seeds of success.

"As a good gardener, you must continuously be on the lookout for weeds. And never allow anyone to plant weeds in your soil. You have the power to determine what goes in your soil. You have the power to decide what goes on in your garden. Make sure to use your power to keep your garden clean. You would never purposely plant weeds in your garden. Always be on the lookout for the negative talk that becomes weeds. Decide right now that you will guard yourself against negative talk.

"All good gardens need three ingredients: rich soil, water, and sunlight. The beauty and the power of this truth is we have more control than we ever imagined. As I've mentioned earlier, the rich soil is your brain. The water is your hard work.

"The final ingredient that you need for your garden to grow is sunlight. In the darkness, nothing grows. In our lives, the sunshine represents hope and attitude. When we have hope and have a good attitude, we can make it. The possibilities are endless. Don't be fooled into thinking that it won't be hard work. Finally, we can have all the sunlight; we can have the best soil and plenty of water. But nothing will grow unless we plant the seed.

"It's important to remember when you remove a weed, that you get all the roots. This can seem like an impossible task. The longer you let the weeds take hold, the longer the roots. We must replace weeds with another thought. When we plant the right seeds in the garden, they can help us defend our entire garden from other weeds. When we pull weeds, it leaves a hole in the ground. It's the same with our lives. If we don't replace and fill in the hole, it just pops up again. With our example of *I'm so stupid*, please, right now, if you have this weed: pull it up! Replace it with *I'm learning something new today, so that I won't make that mistake again.* But we will talk more about this next time.

"Look at me rambling on,' said the farmer. 'I can't reiterate enough. You have the power to stop any weed from gathering in your garden. Don't let anyone have permission to plant weeds without your consent. The beauty of being in control of your garden is you are in control.

"Many people are unhappy and unsatisfied because they have allowed someone to tell them a half-truth, they took the half-truth and planted it in their garden, and after time, it became as large as Jack's beanstalk. Even if you have a weed as big as Jack's beanstalk, you still have an ax to cut it down. The beauty is you get to decide what stays and what goes."

"I would like you to put some of these things into action.'

"I was eager to start and said, 'Let's do it.'

"The farmer smiled and told me he wanted me to decide what I wanted to plant in my garden. No limits, no planning; just what I wanted, and I was to think big. He also wanted me to do this for my life. I looked at him a little cross-eyed. It makes perfect sense to do it for my garden, but for my life?

"The farmer chuckled and asked me to dream about what I wanted for the upcoming year. He wanted me not to only dream about it, to write it down as vividly as I could. Every detail was important. No limits. If nothing was an obstacle, what would I want?

"This is becoming more than what I had expected. How did trying to learn about gardening become about reaching goals and a better life? I said I would try. His face frowned for the first time. He squinted his eyes and said, 'Don't try: Do or do not. There is no try."

"'Was that Yoda you just quoted?'

"His face softened, and he smiled and said, 'Yes. It's a great quote. Trying is what people say when they haven't bought into an idea. It's a way for them to fail without genuinely testing the truth. If you're going to try and not do, you'll be wasting both of our time. I don't say this to be hurtful. I say it from experience. Once you do it, I would love to meet with you again in two weeks. Will you do it?'

"I was excited and scared all at the same time. What if I wasn't smart enough? What if I get it wrong? What if my dreams were too big, and I never achieved them? Or worse, what if they were too small? I could feel the doubt building up in me.

"The farmer said, 'I have trust in you, and I see the seeds of success in you. You just haven't planted them yet. I will see you in two weeks.'

"Jack, I want to tell you the same thing; I see the seeds of greatness in you. You just haven't planted them yet. Will you do what the farmer asked me to do?"

Jack stammered and almost said he would try but caught himself and said out loud, "Do or do not. There is no try."

That night Jack went home and talked with Diane. Luckily, the neighbors weren't home, and they had some peace and quiet. Jack shared the story about the old farmer. He shared what the boss had said, that he saw real potential in him.

Diane smiled and said, "I've been telling you that all along."

Jack just rolled his eyes and kept going.

"The farmer talked about the four seasons every year. And that winter wasn't the time for resting. It was a time for dreaming; that it was vital for us to decide what we wanted in our garden."

Diane stopped him.

"We don't have a garden. We don't even have a yard. And what does a farmer know about getting what he wants?"

"Hold on a second, and I'll tell you. The boss started telling me about his journey, and yes, he called it a journey. You know the boss is very successful, at least it seems that way to me. I think it's worth a try at the very least." Jack caught himself and said out loud, "Do or do not. There is no try."

Diane said, "Did you just quote Yoda?"

They both started to laugh. And then they heard the neighbors come home and turn on the stereo, which only made them laugh even harder.

"Yes, I quoted Yoda. But the boss said that we are giving ourselves an excuse for why something won't work when we say try. Instead of trying, we have to test the idea. Not all suggestions work at the time of testing, usually because we aren't ready for the truth. But more likely, they don't work because we give up before they can work. I'm intrigued to find out if knowing what we want will get us any closer to getting what we want. The more I talk with the boss, the more I am dissatisfied with where we are at in life. I want more for us. What if it's true? There may be greatness in me, and us. I want to reach my full potential."

Diane's eyes started to tear up. She knew that Jack had it in him. Would this be the catalyst to move him forward? For the first time in a long time, she had hope.

Jack's Journal

-Winter time is for Dreaming about what you want
_Our Brains are the rich soil
-Failure is not a definition
-We should test things like scientists
-No "try" do or don't do
-Weeds are based on lies and half-truths
-Brain=the rich soil
-Water=your hard work
-Sunshine is your attitude ★

HOPE LOST

The next couple of evenings, Jack and Diane got online and started looking at houses. At first, they weren't sure what kind of home they wanted or even where they wanted to live. They just started looking, and it was fun and thrilling to think about where they might live someday. They tried not to look at the prices, but it was impossible. The prices seem so high. The more they looked, the more the creeping doubt slipped into their thoughts.

Diane said, "I don't want to look tonight."

And then the room got very cold. Jack knew this meant something was up. He was almost too afraid to ask, but he knew if they were going to move forward with this test of truth. He would need to know why Diane wanted to stop.

"Sweetheart, what's going on? Why don't you want to look anymore?"

Diane started to cry. Big elephant tears began streaming down her face.

"This seems cruel. Look at these homes. Even the ones we don't want seem way out of our price range. I don't see how going through this will help us. I'm so glad the boss sees greatness in you, but how can this get us anywhere? He doesn't know our story. He doesn't know where we have come from. He has no idea about all the disappointments. I'm not sure I can do this anymore. It's so much easier not to dream and not be disappointed. What if we picked the house and found out we can never get one? Won't that even set us back further. It just seems too far away."

Jack's heart swelled. He, too, had let worry and the sheer enormity of getting a house become a giant monster. As he was pondering what to say to Diane to make her feel better. He remembered about the Grand Canyon.

He said, "It's like jumping the Grand Canyon in one leap."

Diane looked at him like he had lost his mind. Wiping the tears from her face, she wondered what the Grand Canyon has to do with us wanting a house. She was ready to lash out at Jack and scream, *That makes no sense!* But instead, she held her breath and waited for Jack to speak.

Jack could see the confused look on Diane's face, so he repeated: "It feels like jumping the Grand Canyon." This made a little more sense to Diane, and she nodded her head.

"The boss talked about this very thing. He said most people see challenges like the Grand Canyon and think you have to leap over it in one giant jump. He told me this is what holds so many people back from even starting to look for what they want. When we decide to start without fear of failure, we find that it's not about the giant leap. It's about small steps done over and over again. When you take this first step, you realize you don't have to jump off the cliff. After the first step, you will see a path that takes you through the canyon, not over it. I know this is scary. But I trust what the boss is telling us. I think we need to push on. Let's dream big and believe. Let's decide what we want."

Diane liked the idea that there was a path to follow that would lead them to get the house they wanted. She tried to envision the path through the canyon. This was going to take real faith. She still had doubt, and she couldn't shake the ominous feeling that they would be disappointed like so many times before. The boss didn't understand. Jack and Diane came from a different world than the boss. It wasn't easy for them. Neither were college-educated. Both came from broken homes. They came from a world that was not kind to them. They had become used to not getting what they wanted. It was their destiny. She decided not to say anything else, but she didn't believe that this would work.

The next morning Diane woke up in a foul mood. She couldn't shake the ominous feeling from the night before. This was going to be one of those days. She started telling herself that it was going to be "a bad day." When she finally decided to get out of bed, she stepped in a puddle of dog pee. Her sock was drenched. She cursed under her breath. Jack probably forgot to take the dog out this morning. She said again, "It's going to be a bad day."

She jumped in the shower and went to wash her hair, but she had no more shampoo. She had forgotten to pick up shampoo last night. Now she was irritated. She had to wash her hair with body soap. This meant her hair would be frizzy all day; what a disaster. She reached for the towel that should be hanging on the towel rack, but it wasn't there. The only towels available were the wet ones from Jack. She couldn't believe how her morning was going. The universe must be against her.

By the time she made it to work, she had cold coffee, she had hit every stoplight, and she had to park out in the boonies. The day didn't get any better from there. The day was a disaster. She secretly thought, *Maybe this is happening because we are trying to get out of our current situation. Maybe God doesn't want us to get what we want. People like us aren't meant to reach our goals. This is a sign. We are meant to be where we are.*

She would talk to Jack when she got home. They needed to stop this foolishness. They had hoped and dreamed for lots of things to see them vanish like the wind. This was a cruel joke that successful people play on the poor and the weak.

I'm not destined for greatness, and even though I love Jack, his greatness is limited. Just look how my day went. I didn't want a bad day. But that's just what I got. Tomorrow probably won't be any better...

By the time Diane got home, she looked like someone had thrown water on her and then tried to steam her dry. Her hair was frizzy, and her makeup was blotchy at best, the vein in the middle of her head was at an all-time high.

As soon as Diane walked into the house, Jack knew instantly that Diane had had one of those days. He knew he needed to tread lightly.

"Rough day?"

"Yes! It started when I stepped in Milo's pee first thing in the morning, and it didn't get any better after that. I knew it was going to be a bad day even before that happened. I even told myself it felt like a bad day. I was right. Nothing went right."

Diane's frustration was growing. Why had the boss set them up for failure? They could never get a house! They didn't make enough money. Homes cost too much in this market. The world is upside down. There is so much unrest in the world. There were homeless people everywhere, wasn't this wrong to want something when so many people were suffering around them? Why did they deserve to have a house? Why did they deserve to have anything? Her whole life had been about lousy timing. This was a bad time to want anything..

Suddenly her mind started to remember everything that she wanted but never got. She was reliving every detail. It all made sense she hadn't achieved what she wanted because she wasn't smart enough. The voice in her head said, *You barely graduated high school. You haven't succeeded because you haven't gone to college. Remember when you only got a C on that chemistry test? Remember when you calculated the checking account wrong and you bounced that check? Remember the embarrassment? That's all because you aren't smart enough to be successful.*

There was a cloud over her head and heart. The voice kept saying, *You can't get a house. You aren't worthy of a home.*

Although Jack couldn't hear the voices in Diane's head, he knew about them. Jack, too, was fighting his demons in his head. These negative voices were a constant battle. He wondered if that was what was going on with Diane. He thought he would talk to her about the garden and how we must protect our garden from weeds. He thought better of it and decided to make dinner and have Diane sit down and relax.

It was nice not to make dinner, even if it was mac & cheese with mini sausages. It was not one of her favorites, but at least she didn't have to make it. Sarcastically, she thought, *Maybe I should want Jack to be a professional chef.* Her face frowned as she thought, *As if.*

After dinner, Jack cleaned up and found Diane sitting on the couch.

"Can I tell you about weeds in the garden?" Diane had a blank stare on her face, but nodded yes and agreement. "I'm not sure I told you about the weeds that we let into our gardens."

Diane responded with, "Yes, you said something about weeds, but I didn't understand. We don't have a garden."

"The garden represents our lives. The garden is how we live. We can have a garden that produces a full crop and yield an incredible harvest, or we can have a garden that yields a few pieces of fruit. The problem is that too many people leave their garden to chance. The boss told me we have a choice of what we plant in our gardens. I'm not exactly sure what he was talking about, but this is what I understand. First, we have a choice, and he emphasized choice in what we let into our garden. All gardens must be protected from weeds. Weeds can choke your plants to death. They take essential nutrients from the ground. They block the sun from helping the plants to grow. We know what weeds look like in our gardens—most of the time. But even weeds can be deceptive in how they look. There are times where weeds may look like flowers. Good gardeners become educated on the plants they want. In life, we, too, have to educate ourselves what the good plants are in our lives.

"From what I understand, the things that we want and the beliefs that we have are the seeds that grow into either weeds of despair or flowers of success. If we plant the right seeds, the seeds of what we want and the seeds of happiness, we will sow a plentiful harvest. Weeds are those negative things that we believe about ourselves. The half-truths that we replay over and over again in our heads. We start to speak these half-truths more out of frustration or disappointment from our past failures. We hear things from family and friends that put doubts about our abilities to be successful. Most people say things not to hurt us but because they're trying to protect us from disappointment. It may be that they see failure all wrong."

Diane now was looking at Jack like he had lost his mind.

"Look at failure wrong? What could you possibly mean? If you fail, you fail. If you make a mistake, there's a price to pay. It's like the kids say, 'It is what it is'… or is it?"

Jack explained, "Our mistakes and failures are not defining unless, of course, you allow those things to define you. Too many times, we look at our mistakes as big life-changing events. At the time of the error, it may even be a doozy. But over our lifetime, there are very few mistakes that we aren't able to come back from. The weeds are those memories of things that went wrong. It's those things that we tell ourselves they are only half-truths. There may be some truth to what we are saying because we've all done stupid things. The key is to be okay with them. To understand it happens to everyone. The odds are, no one will remember them except you. When we plant weeds in our garden, we keep playing them over and over again. It is like going to a lousy movie and re-watching it over and over again. Like that movie you like so much, *Sharknado*."

Diane finally laughed. She started to soften. She was very curious about the weeds. She wanted to know how you get rid of the weeds.

"How do you prevent them from restarting?"

Jack stopped her, "I don't have all those answers yet, but I will ask the boss about them. It may be the next step in getting what we want. It is something I want us to consider. I want us to measure any time we feel like we are letting weeds grow. Do you remember Tom, the guy I used to work with who retired recently?"

Diane nodded her head. He used to quote Zig Ziglar, "Stop the stinking thinking." I believe that actual quote is:

We all need a daily checkup from the neck up to avoid stinkin' thinkin,'
which ultimately leads to hardening of the attitudes.
— Zig Ziglar

"I wonder if that's what he was talking about. Let's try to catch ourselves doing stinking thinking."

Diane snorted a little at the thought. She was willing to try. It sure was better to think about what might be instead of thinking about all the reasons why they wouldn't get there.

"Every time we start to feel that sinking feeling, let's write it down."

Jack agreed this would be the action they would take the rest of the week.

"I think we will take the night off from looking at houses online. But I want us to dream about what we want in a house, what color it will be, what features it will have. This will help us narrow down what we want. You make a list, and I'll make a list. Tomorrow night, then, we will compare our list."

* * * TRUTH * * *

Belief in the truth can be challenging. Believing that greatness starts with a small step can be hard to imagine. We often see the results from people who have made it before us. Not being there the whole way may lead us to believe that greatness happens in 30 minutes or two hours. That's what Hollywood has taught us, even though we know the story may have taken years to be lived. We see it all in two hours.

Each story starts with a person deciding what they want. Sometimes it begins with them deciding what they don't want. They decide they have had enough of the ordinary, and they strive for better—one step, one day at a time.

Jack's Journal

-We control the weeds
-We attract what we believe
-Failure is not permanent
-Success doesn't happen all at once
-Small steps *

IT'S AN ADVENTURE

It had been two weeks since Jack and his boss had met. They were not able to meet last week because the boss had been called away on an emergency. Jack was excited to talk with him about the struggles that he and Diane were having with the concept of knowing what you want. He hoped the boss would have the answers. After the first meeting, Jack reflected on the farmer's story and how starting your day early seems to give you a leg up. He felt like more truths were being emphasized than just what the boss had pointed out. This time he brought a pen and a notebook. He wanted to make sure he wrote everything that the boss shared. On the first page of his notebook, he wrote these four statements.

Here's what I asked:
Here's what you said:
Here's what I did:
Can I ask you more questions?

He was prepared. He made sure that he was 15 minutes early for his appointment with the boss. He sat outside his office and went over his notes. He had asked about why knowing what you want is so important. The boss shared that knowing what you want is the first step to getting it. It's important to imagine it, feel it, and see it in all its glory. The boss shared about the farmer and how knowing what you want in your garden helps you keep out all the weeds. This part was still unclear. *I hope to ask more,* he thought. The boss also talked about time. This was a subtle message.

The way we spend our time defines who we are.
—Jonathan Estim

Jack wanted to know more about this "Truth of Time." He kept going back to the Bible verse that said "there is a time for everything…" He had hoped he'd caught onto one of the secrets that was so obvious. It was nice that he was here 15 minutes early. He smiled and wondered if he was starting to change. He already felt more confident; he still had questions about time, but that might be a part of his journey. He found himself being more curious. For the first time, he felt like he was on a journey to success. The boss greeted Jack with a hardy handshake and a hug, and Jack was taken aback by the gesture.

"So how goes it? Are you finding things that you want? How goes the journey?"

"Diane and I are still working through the first step. It is fun and scary all at the same time." Jack then went through the four statements that he'd written down in his notebook. He explained what he had heard. He talked about the struggles that he and Diane had with this truth and their steps to work through it.

The boss nodded, smiled, and kept his attention entirely on Jack. This made Jack feel important and understood. He didn't interrupt; he didn't fiddle with his phone; and he didn't tap on his computer. He intently listened. Later, Jack wondered if this might be another secret that he had missed. When Jack was done, he said, "This feels like a new journey. A journey I didn't even know existed."

The boss was so pleased to hear him say that. He clapped his hands and stood up and knocked over his chair, and yelled, "Yes! A famous Chinese proverb says: 'When the student is ready, the teacher will come.' You didn't know it, but you were ready. You just needed a little nudge. My wife and I call it an adventure. You never know what will come, what experiences you will encounter, who you will meet. If you can remind yourself it is an adventure, all of life's trials will seem less defining and more about learning."

Jack liked the idea of adventure. But he needed clarification.

"Can you help me understand this adventure ideology? I was just getting my head around the journey."

The boss's eyes gleamed with excitement.

"I like the idea of going on a journey. Sometimes, a journey can seem boring, tedious, and it can become difficult to see where the journey will take us. The journey sometimes doesn't go as planned. It can be easy to get caught up in the moment and lose sight; that whatever happens is just a drop in the bucket of time. There are valleys and mountains on every journey. The adventure word helps me and my family remember that the valleys in life add to the journey, they don't take away. People become so frightened of the valleys that they try to avoid them at all costs. I don't want you to think I'm some religious zealot because I'm not. I believe in truth, and I believe the Bible is transcribed with more truth than any book written. I'm not afraid to share what God has written. I hope this does not offend you. It concerns me when the Bible offends people. Most people aren't offended by the Bible but by people who preach to them. I promise not to preach, but I will share."

> *For whosoever shall be ashamed of me and my word,*
> *the Son of Man will be ashamed of them.*
> — Luke 9:26

"Even back in King Solomon's time, he understood that we must walk through the valley along our journey."

> *Yea though I walk through the valley of the shadow of death, I will fear no evil....*
> — Psalms 23:4

"This is a symbolic description of the word meaning darkness and death, our symbolic valleys on Earth one must walkthrough; that is part of the human experience. The valleys are part of the experience. How we treat the valley is the key to what I like to call the adventure."

Jack nodded in agreement, but he was still uncertain of what this had to do with the adventure. His puzzled look gave him away.

The boss, seeing the concern on Jack's face, shared his story.

"About eight years ago, we planned a trip to Disneyland with the family. We decided it would be more affordable if we drove instead of flying. *Make it an adventure*, is what we thought. We planned to leave Wednesday morning and drive for two days to make it to Disneyland by Friday. Spend the weekend at Disneyland and go down to San Diego for a couple of days before heading home. It was a great plan, but we changed it on a whim. On Tuesday night, we were all packed and ready to leave first thing in the morning. The more I thought about it, the more I like going right now. This is my personality type. It drives my wife crazy at times. But we'll talk about that at a later date.

"So, we hopped in the car with the kids in their pajamas and took off. Not five minutes passed, and my youngest daughter got car sick. I realized that I had not reserved a room for us to stay on Tuesday night. There are six people in our family, so that isn't an easy task, but we went for it anyway. We were able to find a room, and the next morning we took off for Sacramento. It was a nice drive. The kids watched videos on our DVD player. You know, the kind that fits in the car stereo? This kept the kids entertained, and it made the trip pleasant.

"We got to Sacramento way ahead of schedule and stopped at Chick-fil-A. I only mention where we ate because this was a real treat since we didn't have any where we lived at the time. Everyone was in a great mood. The hotel had a pool, so the kids were biting at the bit to go swimming. However, I had forgotten to pack my memory card reader. I knew that I needed to purchase one, and I'd seen a Best Buy down the road from our hotel. This is where the adventure started.

"We pulled into the parking lot of the Best Buy, and we all got out of the car. We were not worried about all of our stuff because the vehicle was locked, and it had an alarm. We had time to kill until we could check in, so we browsed the whole store and stretched our legs. I found a memory card reader, and we purchased it and walked out to the car. When we got to the car, the lock on my driver's side door had been punched out. Someone had broken into our car. They stole our stereo with the DVD player and punched my Chick-fil-A sweet tea cup; tea was everywhere. They ripped the dash pretty good, getting the stereo out. My wife and I had left all our cash for the trip in her purse right next to her seat. My camera and laptop were right behind my seat, not to mention all of our luggage. We couldn't believe it, we only been in the store for 30 minutes. We called the police and spoke to the store manager and were told there was nothing they could do. Was our whole vacation ruined? This was not the adventure we had hoped for.

"As we took inventory of our car. We found that they didn't take the purse filled with cash and credit cards. My briefcase with my laptop and camera was still where I left it. All they took was the car stereo with the DVD Player. We lost the movie Aladdin, but that was it. We were all a little shaken and felt violated. I could feel the mood change. Would we let this one situation ruin our whole trip? No. This was part of the adventure.

"So, I changed the perception of what happened. My wife caught on quickly and jumped aboard. I asked the kids what we could be thankful for in this given trauma. At first, it was a struggle. The age range was 14, 10, six, and three. They didn't see any positives in the situation.

So, my wife prodded them along. She asked if they were missing anything? They all looked around, and all of the stuff they had brought for the trip was still there. The mood was starting to change. She told them that the bad guys didn't get our money that was in the car; that meant we were still going to have a great time at Disneyland. I told them that my camera and laptop were not stolen either. The only thing we lost was the stereo and DVD player.

"'Yeah, but what are we going to do the rest of the trip?'

"I smiled and said, 'I guess we have to go old-school and talk and play road games along the way. This just adds to our adventure. This is a great life lesson.' They all rolled their eyes. Even the three-year-old. 'Your grandma used to say to me, *It builds character*. I used to hate it when she said that, but it was true.

"Not everything in life goes as planned. It's how we perceive what happens. That is the key to success and happiness. I'm not sure that they understood, but the mood changed. When my wife reminded them that we were going swimming, they all smiled at each other. And we said, 'Just another part of the adventure.' The rest of the trip went on without it any real issues. The memorable part is, it made the trip better. We laughed, talked, and played games. To this day, the kids still talk about that adventure, plus I did manage to get another beloved Chick-fil-A sweet tea, too, so all was not lost.

★ ★ ★ TRUTH ★ ★ ★

You can take anything in life and make it seem good or bad. When you find yourself in the valley of your journey, remember it's an adventure. When in the valley, look for something good—anything good—to help bring you through it.

Have a mindset of gratitude. When in the valley, take time to access all the things you have to be thankful. Start a gratitude journal. Science is showing doing a gratitude journal will start to change how your brain is wired.

Start today. In the morning write three things that you are thankful for and three things before you go to bed. Test it!

Jack was pleased to hear the story. It put things into context. Life wasn't all about sunshine and rainbows.

"So, what you are saying is this journey of ours will be filled with valleys. Things will come that we don't expect. We may not even have the tools at the time to deal with them. The valley may seem overwhelming at times. It sounds like we have a choice. To look at the valleys as a complete failure or understand the valleys are just a moment in time. It seems to me that you could have dwelled on your experience and let it ruin your whole vacation. But you choose to see what you still had. I guess you were giving thanks. You didn't spend time blaming anyone or anything. You accepted that it happened and didn't let it define the entire journey. And finally, you kept moving. You didn't give up."

The boss hadn't thought of it that way, but Jack was correct. The key to every journey is first to understand it will be an adventure. Success and failure are genuinely a part of the equation of life. The outcome is not over until your last breath.

"My grandmother told me a story of two frogs that had accidentally fallen in a vat of cream," explained the boss. "My grandmother was from the era of making your own butter. These two frogs jumped into a large vat of cream. Both frogs were able to float for a little while. But it was getting harder and harder to stay afloat. The first frog said: 'This is hopeless.' He tried jumping out of the vat, but it was too high and slippery. Again, he said, 'It is futile.'

"The other frog seeing that you couldn't jump out of the vat, started kicking. The first frog asked, 'What are you doing? You can't kick your way out. You are splashing me, making it hard for me to stay afloat. This is pointless.' But the second frog chose not to listen, and he just kept kicking and kicking and kicking. The first frog gave up and sunk to the bottom of the vat. The second frog kicked so much that he kicked up a small ball of butter to float on. The lady of the house came out and found the frog floating on some of the butter in the vat and scooped him out.

"The moral of the story: There's always a way out. Don't listen to the naysayers. Just keep kicking."

Jack's Journal

−Make like an adventure
−Valley come to everyone−choose to find the good
−Keep kicking ★

STAYING IN THE VALLEY

Jack could see that they were out of time. He had been focusing on the value of time, so he made sure to end the meeting on time.

"Next week, I'd like to talk about the value of time. Is that okay?"

The boss smiled and said, "That would be great. Time is a critical element of any adventure. Next week, I would like you to keep a journal of your time. Every time you start something, write it down. And then record how long you spend on each item. This is the first significant step in understanding the value of time. We will talk about the value of time and the best way to manage it next week." And then the boss did the weirdest thing, he put his hands together, brought them to his heart, and said: "Namaste."

Jack blinked twice and left the boss's office. That was a great meeting; he just wasn't sure about the "namaste" part.

That night, Jack wrote in his journal. So much still to learn. The boss kept telling him it was not a secret. It was just truths we have not recognized. Jack asked the boss why these truths seemed hidden from us. The boss said it was because of our pride. We humans love to make things difficult. When we humble ourselves and sit quietly, these truths can hit us like a ton of bricks. He suggested that Jack take five minutes today and just breathe. When we quite our minds and just breathe we will start to notice the things around us. The truth of this universe starts to become clear. We need to see all its beauty and all the great science that makes up this world. We should always be in awe and humbly understand that we know very little about this universe. When you are able to do that, the truths start coming at you fast.

The boss was very observant. He said, "I see that you have a notebook to take notes. Take it with you everywhere. When you aren't sure what to do. Write the question down. You'll be amazed when you write the question down how your subconscious will start working on it. And eventually, the answer will come. Take time every day to humble yourself and know that the path isn't always clear."

Jack loved the wisdom. He was excited, and yet doubt still crowded his brain. It seemed with every new truth that he learned and mastered—mastered wasn't what he meant…put into practice—it opened up a whole new set of questions and truths. At times, it seemed overwhelming. He decided this might be the valley. The valleys in our lives are only temporary unless we choose to stay there. At first, that statement confused him. Why would anyone want to stay in the valley?

Jack started to write more in his notebook. The boss said, "People hate change. People don't realize there is a path that leads to the mountains. They convince themselves that the valley is all there is. They never choose what they want."

Our greatest fear is not that we are inadequate. Our deepest fear is that we are powerful beyond measure. It is our light, not our darkness, that most frightens us. We ask ourselves, who am I to be brilliant, gorgeous, talented, fabulous? Actually, who are you not to be? You're playing small does not serve the world. We were born to make and manifest the glory of God that is within us. And as we let our light shine, we unconsciously give other people permission to do the same. —Marianne Williamson

In the quiet of the night sitting in his "thinking chair," more and more of what the boss talked about came to mind. How did he miss it the first time? Jack's mind went over every detail of the conversation. He replayed every bit that the boss told him about the valley.

"When people know what they want, the valley becomes part of the adventure, not the journey's end. Every valley teaches us something if we have the right mindset. Did you play any sports as a kid?"

Jack played all the sports, basketball, soccer, baseball, and football.

"Did you win every game?"

"No." Jack thought for a bit. He hadn't won every game. He had a few trophies from times that he did win, but he lost more than he won.

"So, what is the point?" Now remembering his comment, Jack was a little embarrassed by his skepticism.

"When we win, we usually don't take notice of why. When we lose, we tend to pick the things that we need to improve. At least, that's what the most extraordinary athletes do. This is one of the truths that many of us miss. Losing is the valley; if you lost a game, and you decide that you weren't going to play anymore, you wouldn't have a very long athletic career."

Jack loved this analogy. It made sense. Losing in sports doesn't mean you're a loser for life. It means that you needed to improve in some areas. Losing, or the valley, opens our eyes to what we need to learn. It humbles us. Jack was furiously writing everything down in his journal. The valleys allow us the opportunity to expand our understanding of the truth. That truth seems just beyond us. Life is a journey, but we can make it an adventure. Change your mindset on failure, and you can change your whole life. Jack was done for the day. He knew that his dream of a better life may be closer than he thought they ever could be.

Jack opened his laptop to look at something a little lighter, and he came across a video from Jocko titled "Good." The video was so good that Jack got out of his chair and grabbed a piece a paper and wrote down the word "Good." No matter the problem, no matter the issue, say, "Good."

When things are going bad, something good is still happening.
We get the opportunity to figure things out. Good!
So, get up, dust off, reload, recalibrate, re-engage, go out on the attack.
Get After it![2.]

Jack was going to use this. He wrote "Good" in his notebook. When we seek, we find.

Jack wondered how this video would be on his must-watch list. He had never heard of Jocko before today. Is it possible when we are searching for the truth, more truths find us? Now his head was spinning. Time to call it a night.

Jack's Journal pg 70

  -Athletes use the valley or losing as a way to improve
    -When we search for truth, more truth finds us
      -The valley is not the end or our adventure
   -When in the valley keep looking towards what you want *

THE WEEDS

Jack was concerned about the weeds. He knew they were a metaphor for something, but he didn't understand the meaning. This concept, this truth, is one of the hardest truths to master. It is a battle that can be won, but the war will always rage on. Jack asked the boss to please better explain the truth about the weeds in our lives.

The boss shared this Native American parable:

> *An old Cherokee is teaching his grandson about life:*
> *"A fight is going on inside me. It's a terrible fight between two wolves. The one wolf eats anger, envy, sorrow, regret, greed, arrogance, self-pity, resentment, lies, pride, ego, and hate. The other wolf eats joy, peace, love, hope, serenity, kindness, truth, compassion, and faith. This same fight is going on inside you and every other person, too."*
> *The grandson thought for a minute and then asked his grandfather, "Which wolf will win?"*
> *The old Cherokee simply replied, "The one you feed."*

"We have a choice which wolf we will feed. I talked with the farmer about the weeds during one of our morning talks. I remember like it was yesterday. I had been visiting the farmer for about three months straight—every Thursday at 6:00 a.m. My routine was set. Every morning, I got up early, meditated, worked out, and then got ready for work. I would arrive early to work, read 25 pages from a self-help book, and then plan my day. My journey seemed to be on an upward trajectory. Then things seemed to go south fast. I was passed over for promotion, and my largest client decided to leave our firm. Mistakes from the past caught up with me financially, and we were in real trouble.

"The spiral wouldn't stop. I started to believe that life was against me. The voices got louder. The ones that tell you there is no way out. That we are destined for failure. All my failures from my whole life started to flood my conscious brain. Every time something happened, I saw the negative. Something as simple as hitting all the stoplights on my way to work was a clear sign of what a loser I was. One thing after another just kept going wrong. I was in the valley, which was way before I realized the truth about valleys and adventures.

"As I said, I was meeting with the farmer. I arrived 15 minutes early, which had become my norm. I sat in my car and tried to pump myself up for the meeting. I reviewed my notes, but it felt like everything the farmer had told me wouldn't work for a guy like me. I was a big fat loser. Look at my history. I wasn't famous, or even successful. I had been a failure at so many things. If I judge myself on my actions, not the intentions, I had failed miserably as a boss, husband, and father. My relationship with God had also faltered. I started to believe a great lie.

"Let me pause here for a second. We have spoken about truths, and that they aren't secrets, we just haven't noticed them. It's like seeing a magic trick, and it all seems mysterious until someone shows us how to do it. The great lies are different. They don't hide from our understanding. They hit us in the face. These great lies always tickle our conscious and subconscious minds. They play on our self-awareness and our lack of self-awareness. They amplify every mistake we make. They tell us that these things define us. They tell us, 'You are all alone. You're the only one who's ever had this problem. Don't share with anyone because they won't understand. People will think that you are deranged and unworthy of their love and friendship. They won't want to help you. You're on your own, and you should be ashamed.'

"The Great Lies make sure we go into a box and hide. It tells us to do our best to hide these mistakes and thoughts: 'Don't let anyone know. The alienation will only get worse if you share.' And these lies become even worse because they are coming at you in your own voice. Why would you lie to yourself? So, we start to believe them. I'm no psychologist, but I sometimes wonder if the spike in depression is because we listen to this inner voice that keeps spewing lies.

"The prime example that I can remember is when I was a newlywed. My wife and I had been married for just under a year. The honeymoon was over, and we were trying to figure out this marriage thing. We would have fights over silly things. We would keep score—just as a side note, never keep score with your wife. She always does more than you think and always more than you. At least in my house— I wouldn't say we were miserable, but it was a rough patch. We had started going to this church, and they created a young marriage group. This was a group of young married couples that would meet once a week and talk about marriage and relationships. It was one of the most eye-opening experiences of my life. Some Great Lies were brought out into the open. I believe 10 couples met with Charlie and Karen Rice in a small group setting. It changed the trajectory of the 10 couples' lives. It has been years now since the group has met.

Of the 10 couples, nine are still married to this date, and they have been married for over 28 years. What was the secret to this group? No secret. We shared our struggles.

"I remember hearing one of the other husbands talk about an issue that he was having. I thought, *Oh my, I have said and thought that very thing.* I wasn't alone. My wife felt the same way. We weren't crazy. Others were having the same problems. This freed us up to deal with the real issues instead of keeping them locked away. If we aren't careful, the great lies will creep back in and convince us that we are all alone. Knowing that other people have the same thoughts and are making the same mistakes opens your heart and mind to new possibilities.

"Back to the farmers' meeting…

"I had lost track of time. With anguish, I couldn't shake that I was stuck and had no way to do anything other than fail. As usual, the farmer had seen me pull up, and he came out on his front porch five minutes before we were to meet. When I didn't get out of the car, he walked to me. I was so engaged in my self-talk, I didn't notice him approaching the car. He knocked on my window with his warm smile, and I think I let out a little yelp. I smiled weakly at him. We walked to his house in silence. I later came to learn the farmer was a bit of an empath. Not anything like a psychic, but an empath; someone who can sense and feel things that other people are feeling. The farmer got me a hot cup of coffee and looked at me like he knew everything I was going through. The warmth and caring was radiating through him. I felt vulnerable. I was a man. I was supposed to have all of this under control. I was a fake. I had nothing under control. On the outside, I put on a mask of happiness and success. But I was buried under my thoughts. It was like the farmer could read my mind.

"'Do you remember when we talked about the weeds in your garden?' he asked.

I couldn't speak. My words were caught in my throat. I was flooded with emotion. I just nodded my head. I was weary, and my notebook just laid in my lap. The farmer seemed to know how I felt and his eyes widened.

"He said, 'I want you to listen, not only with your ears. I want you to listen with your heart, soul, and mind. When we tend to our garden, it is a constant battle to check for weeds. New gardeners don't always catch the weeds early enough. The fact is, they don't know how a weed should look. We sometimes get fooled into thinking they are a plant that will bear great fruit. Sometimes, the seeds we plant accidentally get plucked from the soil because they look like weeds. We can inadvertently pluck the wrong things, and then we don't have a garden full of beautiful vegetables but a garden full of nasty weeds.'

"The farmer paused, and let it sink in.

"'Our thoughts and attitudes can either be the seeds that yield a beautiful harvest or be the seeds of disaster. We decide. There is no garden without weeds. It's natural. We live in a world of weeds. I've been told in the early days of man. We needed to remember negative things. More important to remember negative things than positive things. Suppose we ate a plant that made us sick. We had to remember not to eat the plant again.'

"I wasn't sure I understood. I looked puzzled, but the farmer was bringing me out of my haze. I no longer was focusing on my failures, but now I was contemplating the meaning of his message.

"'If we hear a particular noise, we need to remember that it was a tiger that ate Uncle John. So next time we heard that same sound, we would turn and run away. This part of the brain is called the amygdala. Considered the oldest part of our brain. This part of our brain would be beneficial if we had to worry about tigers and what not to eat. But today, we don't very often come across a tiger that wants to eat us. We do still hold on to those negative thoughts, though. These negative thoughts are the things we tell ourselves about ourselves that aren't true. They are things we tell ourselves that are only half-truths. They are things that we may have done, they may be failures, but we allow them to become more significant and more frightening. We see these failures as a defining moment. We allow these memories to make giant leaps that lead us in the wrong direction. These thoughts, these weeds take over. These weeds make us believe that past mistakes mean a future of failure. The cloud becomes a storm and then the storm becomes a hurricane. We need a way to stop this.

"'Have you ever wondered how these negative thoughts can get started? Our brains are marvelous machines. Our thoughts engrave deep passageways through our brains. It makes it easy for us to remember things and do things. Most people call these things habits. These pathways become deeper and more defined the more we think a thought or say a phrase. It becomes easier and easier to recall a feeling, an idea the more we focus on it.

"'It's like we all have a stone tablet in our lives. At the start, we scribble our thoughts and our feelings on the tablet with a light pen. The more we do something or think something, the deeper the writing gets on the tablet. Finally, if you believe something long enough, you chisel those words, so they become permanent. They could be good words. They could be bad words. But we all do it. Have you ever wondered why sometimes things happen that stick with you longer than others? Have you ever wondered why it's so much easier to take criticism to heart and dismiss praise?'

"I just nodded my head. I could feel that the farmer was speaking real truth. I was so intrigued that I was sitting on the edge of my seat. The farmer could tell I was eager to learn more.

"'The answer lies in the words that you have chiseled on your stone tablet. These words become the seeds of weeds. When someone uses words of praise, and you don't have those words imprinted on your tablet, you believe them to be false, and you downplay the significance of those words. In essence, you don't let the good seeds ever take root.

"'On the other hand, because we have these words of defeat chiseled into our stone tablets, every time someone criticizes us or says something to help us improve, we only hear the negative. It's like the words on the tablet get red hot and start flashing. All the meaning that we have associated with that word comes rushing in. With the rush comes all the seeds of doubt. With every doubt comes another doubt, and then you find yourself reliving failures or at least perceived failures from the last 20 years. If we don't have any way to stop the voices, they will carry us down a path of self-destruction.'

"The farmer stopped and looked deep into my eyes. 'Stop now!'

"I blinked, and a look of confusion covered my whole face.

"'Stand up.' He said, 'I want you to put your arms out like you are playing airplane with your kids.' I did what he asked, but I was perplexed. 'On the count three, I want you to clap your hands together, and when you clap, I want you to say: *Stop!*

"I put my hands out, and when he counted to three, I brought them together and said, 'Stop!' We did this three times. I'm not sure why, but it made me feel a little better.

"'I learned this little technique from Anthony Robbins. Years ago, I went to one of his seminars, and he said we need a way to stop the negative voices in our heads. The only way to get them to stop is to tell them to stop. Clapping your hands is the action part. The sting of clapping your hands lets your brain know you are serious. The only way to get out of the weeds is by action. Clapping your hands is the action. Saying stop is the command. Test it. Every time you hear those voices tell you, you can't do something. That you are a loser, that you are not smart enough, too old, too young, too poor... You get the point. Put your arms out and clap your hands and say stop.'

"I laughed and said, 'I might do this all day. But I can't walk around clapping and saying stop all day. People will think I'm crazy.'

"'This may be true. Find a time to do it when you are alone. Over time, you'll be able to set the trigger to make the weed stop growing. Knowing how to get the weeds to stop talking to you is the start, but if you don't replace the weeds with the seeds of success and happiness, the weeds will just come back even stronger.'

"'That makes perfect sense but are those weeds or evil voices lying? They are telling me or at least reminding me that I am not perfect. Aren't they helping me stay humble? Aren't I suppose to be humble? Don't they help me improve?'

"The farmer nodded and grunted, 'Staying humble is important. In the grand scheme of things, you are correct. We know very little, and failures are a steppingstone to our success. Unfortunately, those voices only tell you half-truths. It is true you have made mistakes. We all have. We also have failures. Look at my favorite president,' as he pointed to the wall and a picture of President Lincoln, 'he failed seven times when he ran for office. I believe he failed the bar exam five times. If he let those seven defeats those seven failures define him, where would our country be now? We might all be speaking German under Nazi rule. But that's for another time.'

"'My point is that these weeds tell us half-truths, only part of the story. They try to convince us that these failures and mistakes are the end of the story. Not just part of the story. If they were there to remind us of what we had learned, then they would be telling us the whole truth. If they told us that it's over, and we must move on to fight another day. Then they would be telling us the entire truth. But they don't. We have to remind ourselves of these things. We need to replace the weeds with the seeds of happiness and success. We need to stop the weeds from blooming and then pluck them out of the ground. We need to look at the words that we have written on our stone tablets and replace them with words of encouragement and affirmation. These are the things that we say out loud over and over again until they burn the weeds to the ground. They make the weed words fade.

"'When I was young, I took a computer programming class in high school. It was based on the old DOS system. One of the first things we learned was how to write the "if-then" statement. They look like this...' The farmer took out a piece of paper and drew out an "if-then" statement.

"'Our brains work like this. When we tell ourselves the negative things, our brains cannot decipher what is real and what we have made up. If we say to ourselves, *I'm so stupid*, this is how the brain processes the statement.'"

"'This simple change is all it takes to change your trajectory. I want you to notice that the language completely changed. I did not say to myself, *I am not stupid*. Our brains don't hear the negative. Don't get confused. Our brains understand negative statements. It doesn't understand a double negative. It does not hear the *not* in this statement. When we plant the seeds of what we want, we only see the result. It's best to start with *I am* statements.'

"The look on my face must've been of someone who had gotten an anonymous call that says you just won $10 million dollars and all they need is my checking account number, routing number, and social security number. I wasn't buying what he was saying. I couldn't stop looking at the farmer with my lemon-eating face. My wife has told me I should never play poker. I don't hide my emotions very well. You can almost always tell what I'm thinking when I'm thinking it.

"'I can tell by your face two things. You don't believe the truth will work, and you are dealing with lots of weeds right now.' My face softened. I no longer looked like I had bitten into a lemon. Now my face just showed despair, worry and fear.

"'All of these worries that you have now, how many are real?' He didn't wait for me to answer. 'This reminds me of a quote from Mark Twain...'"

I have been through some terrible things in my life, some which actually happened.

"'Weeds convince us that we are living through terrible things. When dealing with worry, we need a trigger to stop the worry. Worry freezes us from taking action. Action is the key to destroying the weeds in our life. When I get frozen by worry, I ask myself these questions:

What is the worst thing that could happen?
Can I survive?
What is the likelihood it will actually happen?
What can I do?
What would I tell a friend to do in the same situation?

"'When you ask these questions, it creates a new pathway in your brain. It makes you stop concentrating on the problem and starts you focusing on the solution. Many times, it shows us that worry is unfounded. When you ask these questions, consider: have you ever gone through a similar situation before? Did you make it through it?'

"'I am so glad that you are journaling. Journaling helps you look back on what you were worried about in the past. It's quite humorous when I look back at my journal and see all the things I was so concerned about. Ninety-nine-point-nine percent of these things never worked out as I had thought they would or imagined. Here's the essential part: even though I worried and let the emotion bog me down, I found it was a wasted emotion to worry. But I had to write them down, so I could deal with them. I did tell myself I would not let worry rule me. I would not let fear guide my life."

★ ★ ★ TRUTH ★ ★ ★
Fear is false evidence appearing real.
False
Evidence
Appearing
Real

"'Stop playing the soundtrack in your head. Pull those weeds. Plant the seeds of success.'

I could feel some of his words were starting to melt my resistance. I was still skeptical about the process.

"'Does this work?' This time I didn't say it to myself; I said it out loud.

"The farmer just nodded his head yes.

If you think you can or can't you're probably right.
—Henry Ford

"I want you to start today. I want you to start telling yourself who you really are. Not the way you think you have been. Our words are so powerful…"

And God said, let there be light, and there was light.
—Genesis 1:3

"I am no biblical scholar, but if God used words and they became, is it possible our words can make us become also? My test of this truth says yes. The seeds we want are the good and worthy things in life. All of these weeds in our garden do nothing for you or anyone else. When we focus only on our weeds, we become sour, self-serving, and reclusive. Tonight, I want you to write three statements about yourself. They all start with *I am*. They all must be positive. I want you to reflect on the weeds you were focusing on and write the opposite statement.'"

"I blinked in disbelief, but nothing the farmer had told me had been false.

"'I just lost one of my biggest clients, and I can't seem to get any more business. I'm not a good business person. I have made so many mistakes. I'm going to lose my job. Lose my house. My wife will leave me. I won't ever be able to pull out of this…' The weeds keep pouring out. I was amazed that I had so many worries pent up in just 10 minutes.

"The farmer jumped up with a smile on his face. He put on his arms and clapped his hands and yelled, 'Stop!' I almost fell out of my chair. My eyes were as big as saucers. He just looked at me and nodded. He made a head motion for me to stand up and do the same thing. I felt foolish, but I did it.

"'I don't usually give anyone their first affirmation, but I'm going to make an exception for you. Write this down in your notebook.'

"I sat down and grabbed my notebook. I wrote down what he said:

"'I am attracting new business relationships every day.'"

"He instructed me to write it 25 times every morning and every night before I went to bed. You need to come up with two more affirmations and do the same thing. Write them on a sticky note, put them on your bathroom mirror, and say them out loud 25 times every day.

I could do this, but man, it seems like a lot of work. What was my wife going to think when she heard me talking to myself? What if I was writing a lie? I was not attracting business to me. How could I write the statement and believe it?

"The farmer could see that I was still down. He continued to explain, 'The thoughts that you have, the weeds you just told me about, are they truly who you are?' Without waiting for my answer, he said, "No, your affirmations are about who you can be, not who you think you are now. *Now* only lasts for a second. You are who you want to be. By saying and writing your affirmations, you tell yourself— which is telling your brain—that you do not accept the weeds. You are what you say you are. When you do this repeatedly, your brain starts to believe it, and it will help you make decisions congruent with your statement. You will be pulling the weeds and filling the holes with the seeds of success.

"'Our time is up.' He smiled and patted me on the back. 'You have greatness in you.'"

Jack was writing so fast that his hands ached. He had written so many notes so quickly, he hoped he could read them. Jack and his boss were out of time too.

"Jack, I want you to do the same thing that the farmer instructed me to do." The boss opened his desk drawer, pulled out a leather-bound notebook, and showed Jack his journal. And it had today's date on the top. There were his three affirmation statements written 25 times. Jack instantly got the point. This wasn't just a story. Before him was a man of action. In fact, this was one of the affirmations written in the boss's notebook: "I am a man of action."

With that, the meeting was over, and the boss said, "Namaste," and for the first time, Jack said it, too.

Jack's Journal

-Start small
-Remove the worry of "active energy"
-Write down vividly what you want
-Say and write your affirmations everyday.*

THE ACTION

The following week, Jack started writing his affirmations every morning. He was up at 5:00 a.m. He had started a routine. Every night, he put his clothes out that he would wear, making sure everything was clean and pressed. He wasn't going to allow "active energy" to hold him back. His morning routine was to get up at 5:00 a.m. and go downstairs and meditate for 15 minutes, a breathing exercise that he saw on YouTube. The author of the urban Monk said that breathing creates energy in the body. He decided to test it; not try. It worked. He felt more energy. He exercised for 15 minutes on the elliptical. It no longer was a clothes hanger. He then had a cup of coffee and just relaxed. He was amazed at how refreshed he felt every day. It was hard at first, but he had been doing it now for about three weeks, and it started to feel like a habit.

Diane was starting to notice the differences. She became inspired to do the same thing. Eventually, the routine would change a little. Jack and Diane would start taking walks together every morning. It helped their communication and was one of the things that they point to today when asked how have they have been married for so long. Thirty years and still counting.

Jack and Diane were still grappling with the idea of knowing what you want. Jack told Diane, "I want a house. I want a home for children. I want a big yard that they can play in. I want a neighborhood with other kids and parents that will become our friends. I want a wrap around the porch. An oversized master bathroom with two sinks and a large shower that will fit two people easily." He smiled and raised his eyebrows up-and-down. Diane liked the house already. "I want a shop so we can work on projects. I want a three-car garage and entertainment room to watch football. I want a fireplace." Diane was getting excited.

Diane started to add the things that she wanted: "I want a big kitchen and dining area, so we can have the family over for the holidays. I want it to be open with lots of windows and natural light. I want a palm tree in the front yard. I want the yard to be landscaped with blooming flowers year-round." And with a big smile, she said, "I want to have a garden."

A wave of hope enveloped Jack and Diane. Jack got out his journal and wrote everything down. It was very exact. Diane asked if she could type up all the details. They would read it every night before they went to bed. A big sigh of relief came over them. After a month and a half, they finally knew what they wanted. Now what? Jack couldn't wait for what to do next.

Jack was starting to see the difference in writing his affirmations every morning and evening. He read them out loud in the bathroom every morning before he went off to work. It was working. Things were starting to change. ✶

TIME TRUTH

For the next seven days, Jack recorded his time. He recorded when he woke up; he recorded everything that he did throughout the day. After the third day, he started to see trends. He spent a lot of time putting out fires. There were a few days that he didn't get done anything that he needed to be done. He noticed when he got home, he ate dinner, helped clean up, and then he watched about five hours of TV a night. If he wasn't watching TV, he was on his phone, reading Facebook. He also noticed that he wasn't spending much time with Diane. He was spending at least 15 minutes a day journaling, and he was proud that he was continuing that habit. The more that he looked at his time log, the more concerned he became about how he was spending his time. He was getting up earlier and had his morning routine down. What was he missing? Jack wasn't sure he could do any more than he was already doing. Most days, he felt like he had no control of his time. He rationalized that the time at home was his. He needed this time to relax and to re-energize himself. The thought had crossed his mind that maybe he should be doing more. But he just didn't have the time.

The week went by extremely fast. He logged his time for four of the seven days. He just didn't have the time to do the other three days. The boss would understand. The date came to meet with the boss.

Jack again was 15 minutes early. He was ready to talk about the truth about the valleys and how he was excited to change his mindset. He had highlighted in his journal, "This is just a moment in time," and "Keep kicking until you have a ball of butter to float on." He and Diane had talked about the ability to look at their successes and failures and dissecting them into two parts. What went well, and how could they repeat it? What went wrong, and what did they learn from it? They talked about not getting bogged down in the valley. Diane even bought two little frogs to put on their keychains to remind them to keep kicking. Diane typed up Marianne Williamson's quote. She would read it out loud every morning before she and Jack went to work. Next to the bed was a list of things that they had wanted for their house. Every night, she read it out loud before they went to sleep. Jack wasn't sure about Diane, but he had had many dreams about that house. He would wake up excited and hopeful.

The boss opened the door and greeted Jack with "namaste" and shook Jack's hand. This was the second time that the boss had used "namaste." Jack looked at the boss quizzically.

"You're probably wondering about the greeting," said the boss. Jack nodded and half grunted a yes.

"As you may know, I'm a chronic reader. I read at least two books a month. This month, one of the books I am reading is *Aspire* by Kevin Hall. He writes about the power of words. The words we use and why they're so important. In the first two chapters, he introduces us to two words, Genshie, and namaste."[3.]

Jack interrupted and said, "Isn't this what hippie yoga people say to each other?" The boss clapped his hands and laughed out loud.

"I'm not sure about the hippie part, but yes, many people that practice yoga greet each other with namaste. Do you know what it means?"

Jack shook his head.

"No, I have no idea."

"I didn't know until I read it in Kevin Hall's book either. I don't have the exact meaning quoted by the author. So, I will paraphrase. it means: I know the God-given talents in you. I know what makes you special, and I honor it."

"I salute the divine within you. I salute what you do best.
I salute your natural gifts I honor your uniqueness and your specialness."[4.]

"You noticed I shook your hand also. Do you know why we shake hands?" Jack had no idea. "That's okay. In Kevin's book, it explains. The handshake is a clear way to show I am not carrying any weapons.

"Namaste carries a message of peace and harmony. I know it's a little different. But I want to be the difference that I hope the world to be. If I seek to honor you first and then you seek to honor someone else, this could start a trend. What if we honor first and stop worrying about what we deserve? How much better would the world be if we decided to serve before being served?

"One of the answers we all are looking for is how to serve better? The key is to recognize the gifts that we have in ourselves. If I focus on your gifts, by which I mean honoring your gifts, I in turn focus on my gifts. The heart of most problems is that we focus too much on ourselves. How it makes us feel. How we been wronged. Why does that person get a new car, but I don't? We judge others on their actions, and yet judge ourselves on our intentions. Each one of us is unique. Not a single duplicate in the world. If I can live my life honoring your uniqueness and your gifts what have I lost? I believe what I gain is everything. By honoring your gifts, by treating you like you are an honored guest, I lift you up. How does that make you feel?"

Jack was so focused on what the boss was saying, he just blinked. He had been writing feverishly in his notebook. This was a good question. How did he feel? Thoughts kept rushing in. He did feel like an honored guest.

He said, "It makes you feel important. Like you matter."

The boss said, "Exactly. This is what namaste means. I want to treat you and everyone I meet like an honored guest. What unique things can I learn from you? What insights do you have on your path that I have not seen yet? This simple word helps me to seek to understand before being understood. Every person I meet, greet, or pass, I think namaste. I may not say it every time, but I think it and whisper to myself."

In Jack's notebook, he wrote the word namaste in bold letters and underlined it three times. Honor those gifts everyone has inside them, even if you can't see them. It reminded him of a Sunday school teacher who said love thy neighbor as thyself. When we honor others' gifts, we also recognize our own.

Jack lifted his head from his notebook, he flipped to the first page to discuss the three statements that he had learned early on in meetings with the boss. The process that he and Diane had gone through to pick out the kind of house that they wanted. Diane had typed it all up, and they were reading it every night. She had also typed up the quote from Marianne Williamson, and they read it every morning. Now came the question of time, was it one of the truths?

"Did you do your time study?" Jack pulled out a piece of paper and gave it to the boss. The boss studied the log. "It looks like you have only four days on here."

Jack nodded.

"I just didn't have the time to do the other three days."

His boss's eyebrows lifted, and he gave Jack a look like Jack's mother used to give him when he was fibbing.

"Jack, I like you. You have great promise. What do you mean you ran out of time?"

Jack knew he had misspoken, but he wasn't sure what he should have said. He looked sheepishly at the boss. After what seemed like an eternity, and yes, Jack did see the irony because it felt like time stood still, Jack gathered his thoughts and finally spoke.

"I guess the more I think about it. It wasn't that I didn't have time; I didn't make time to do what I was going to."

The boss smiled. "You just officially learned one of the truths."

★ ★ ★ TRUTH ★ ★ ★

We make time for things we believe are important to us. The key to using time to your advantage is to decide if what you are doing is leading you towards what you want or away from it. If it's not moving you towards it, then in all probability it is moving you away from it. Time stands still for no one. It is the great equalizer.

Jack was surprised. He grabbed his notebook and started writing down what the boss just said. We have the time and make the time for things we want to do.

"How does that work? I don't think I purposely didn't keep records of my time because it wasn't important."

The boss shrugged his shoulders. That may be the case, but I can assure you if you wanted it bad enough, you would have made sure that you took the time to get it done. Here's how I know: we always make time for the things we want to do.

"It's been about 10 years ago I was on my way home from work. My wife called me and asked if I would stop and pick up a gallon of milk. It was on my way home, and it wouldn't have taken me more than about five minutes. It had been a long

59

day, and I was tired, and I just wanted to get home. That five minutes felt like it would take hours, I pleaded with her to just let me come home. My wife was very understanding and said, 'Okay, just come home.' I barely hung up when my phone rang again. It was my best friend and he had just flown into town. He wanted to know if I would meet him at the club and get a round of golf in.

"'Heck yeah,' I said, 'that would be great I need to stop at the house grab my clubs and then I would meet him there in about 20 minutes.' I hung up the phone. I had new energy: I was excited to get to go play golf, and I just found two hours. That's when it dawned on me, why is it that I didn't have five minutes to pick up milk but I had an extra two hours to go play golf?"

Jack's eyes lit up. He interrupted the boss.

"It's because you make time for the things you want to do."

"Exactly! At the same time, I came to this realization I was driving past the grocery store. I pulled in the store and picked up the milk and some flowers. I called my friend back and told him I was going to pass on golf. I went home apologize to my wife and decided then and there that I was going to do what needed to be done before I did the things that were fun.

"Time is the great equalizer. No one gets more than 24 hours a day. Our time here on the planet is limited. Do you manage your time, or does time manage you? For most people, management of time seems tedious. At the end of the day, we don't account for what we did. Did we get done what needed to get done? Did we get done what we wanted to do? Did we move closer to what we wanted or further away? Time does not stand still for anyone. I read online about a study of retired business people; it said their number one regret was they wished they had done more with the time that they had. That they wished they had spent more time working on the important things and had spent more time with their family and friends.

"The time log is vitally important. If we don't know what we are spending our time on, how will we know if we are spending it wisely? This leads us back to knowing what you want. If we don't know what we want, we cannot dedicate time to it. We are either moving towards our goal or away from it. There is no middle ground. Time does not pause. If you are not moving towards what you want, time will move it farther away. We can never catch up for the lost time. The beauty of time is, even though we can never make up for lost time, we can put time to good use."

Jack thought for a moment. Was he moving towards his wants and goals? Was he wasting valuable time? Jack knew that he wasted some time goofing off, but wasn't this good, too? All work and no play makes Tom a dull boy. Jack loved to play. Was this good for you?

Almost like the boss could read his mind, he went right into that subject.

"Jack, did you know that the average father only spends five minutes a week talking with his children? The average CEO only spends six minutes talking with his employees." Jack shook his head. How much time had he spent with his employees? Six minutes a week? He wasn't sure he had even spent that much time.

"Oh crap!" He whispered out loud.

The boss just smiled.

"On the four days that you did log your time, how much time was spent talking and building your relationship with Diane? Don't answer. How much time did you spend helping your employees? Time is so fleeting that a day can go by in a blink. A year can seem like a heartbeat. Make time a priority. Schedule your fun, plan date nights, plan on meeting with your employees regularly. Plan to spend time on self-growth. It is good to have well-rounded goals. You would never just plant one vegetable in your garden. You plant a variety as you grow and expand your horizons. The best way to spend your time is to do what needs to get done first.

"Many 'time gurus' say do what you don't want to do first and get it out of the way. I want you to keep a time log for two weeks. I want you to understand how you are spending your time. This is the only way that you will ever know if you have the time to accomplish what you want. How you spend your personal time is not for me to judge. That is up to you to decide. Finding the greatness in you takes effort, hard work and time.

"After the first week, look to see if there are any trends. Compare your time log to the things that you needed to get done. Compare it to the things you wanted to get done. How did it compare? Were you able to take time to be with your wife, your kids? What did you do for yourself? How much time did you spend on personal growth? How much time did you spend on the really important things? The time log will help you see what you're spending your time on. How we spend our time is a habit. Habits are very useful. It is the way that our brains allow us to get things done without using a lot of energy. If we aren't careful these time habits can lead us to nothingness. The time log challenges us to reassess how we spend our time and make sure that we are using time for the things we want and not to fritter it away.

Jack looked up from his notebook.

"Man, you are so right when you told me it all starts with what I want. If I don't know what I want, how will I know if I'm spending my time correctly? I know what you want from me; I know what the job needs from me, most of the time, but I'm not sure that I spend my time on what's most important. It feels like I spend a lot of time putting out fires. I need to spend time to decide what I want for every aspect of my life. If I have a point that I'm aiming for, I will then be able to decide how much time to spend on each item."

The boss was pleased.

"I think you're starting to get it. It's easy to see what it takes to move forward. Much harder to do. When you know what you want, you can start using the time to your advantage. When I did this exercise for the first time, I was amazed at how little time was spent in relationships that I valued. I was amazed at how little time I spent on my physical health. It was an eye-opener: I spent most of my time on nothing. I was so selfish with my downtime. I can be an incredible time-waster.

Hours upon hours of mindless activities. The funny thing is, I always felt horrible about wasting this time. Somehow, I knew that I wasn't being productive. Don't get me wrong; I'm not talking about working 80 to 100 hours a week. I'm talking about doing things that help build relationships, that build our personal growth for a better tomorrow. Play games with your children, take your wife out on a date, read a book to further your understanding of life. Plan your downtime. Don't just do mindless activities. They rob you of so much, and they can easily become a habit and rob you of the most valuable things you possess."

Jack understood now. It wasn't that he couldn't do the things that he enjoyed, like watching TV at night or playing golf. It meant he needed moderation. He needed to set limits. Everything you spend time on can rob time from something else. How we use time can and will become a habit. Don't let the habit of wasting time lead you away from what you want. Jack decided to dedicate himself to spend time doing his "time log" for the next two weeks. He told the boss he understood, and he would do the two-week log starting today. He decided that he would use the Law of Intentionality from John Maxwell's book, *The 15 Invaluable Laws of Growth*:

Growth, doesn't just happen. Growth must be intentional.

"You are correct," said the boss, "We need to decide what we need to do and then set a time that we will do it. Without having a set time, we will let "active energy" slow us down. This is especially important when you are starting a new routine. Set the time now. What time will you start your time study?"

Jack did his best "thinking man" pose and said, "It's now 10:00 a.m., I will go back to my desk and at 10:15 start my time log. Every morning at 7:00 a.m., I will start the next day's time sheet."

The boss smiled.

"Jack, one last thing before we end today. I want you to be a man of action. I want you to do what you say you will do. No exception. If you can do this very important action, people will follow you to the end of the Earth."

⋆ ⋆ ⋆ TRUTH ⋆ ⋆ ⋆

Character is important. People judge you by your actions. Do what you say you are going to do. No exceptions; no excuses. Nothing will turn people off more than not being a person of your word.

Jack went back to his office and laid out his time log. As he was pondering everything that the boss had said, he realized that he was already doing some of the things to help his time work for him. He had started this morning routine: getting up early, meditating, reading, and exercising. These simple activities were making him feel better about the day. He knew if he didn't start his time log now, it would be harder to do it tomorrow. He was reading every day now. Even though the boss hadn't talked about reading, he had noticed all the books in the boss's library. He took it on himself to pick a book at random, buy it, and start reading it.

The first book he picked was *15 Invaluable Laws of Growth* by John Maxwell. John talked about the law of diminishing intent:

> *The longer you don't do something you should do now,*
> *the greater the odds that you will never actually do it.* [5.]

He knew from experience this was so true. He promised to be, a man of action. He continued to make his time log. He also started writing down the things that were important to him, the things that he wanted.

After about 30 minutes, he had a time log designed, and he started using it immediately. He would never again say he was going to do something and not do it. He wrote in big, bold letters: **Do it now!**

He smiled and got on about his day.

Jack's Journal

-You are either moving towards your goals
or away from them
-Time is the great equalizer
-Do what you say you are going to do
-Be a man/person of action
-You get what you measure
-Time log helps you see where you spend your time
-Have a plan, set a time that you will start *

SPRING

Jack went home to Diane. He pulled out his notebook and read Diane his notes on the meeting with the boss. He also stopped and logged the time that he was spending with her. Diane loved the idea of date night once a week. She asked if he minded if she did a time log also. She asked if he would share his, so she could use it. As Jack was flipping through the pages, Diane noticed that there were three pages of the same thing written over and over again.

"What is that?"

Jack blushed, "Those are my weed killers."

Diane knew by now it was best not to judge until she heard the rest of the story. The boss had some pretty "out there" concepts, and she'd been skeptical from the start, but they seemed to be making a change in Jack. So, she wanted him to explain.

"You know I told you about the farmer and the boss."

Diane nodded; she hoped someday she would be able to meet the man who had influenced the boss and her husband. He was creating quite a legacy.

"Yes, I remember you told me about him."

"Do you remember he talked about the seasons in the year?"

Diane paused to gather her thoughts.

"Oh yeah, I remember the wintertime is for dreaming about or deciding what we want to put in our garden. This means this is the time where we decide about wanting a house with a big yard where we decided that we want to start a family."

Jack said, "Exactly, wait what?"

Diane's face lit up, and tears came streaming down her face.

"I went to the doctor today. We are going to have a baby."

Jack jumped up and kissed her. They danced around the apartment ironically with the loud music from the neighbors above them. Their excitement was over the top. Jack sat back down.

"It's when you decide what you want and who you want to be, that starts everything." She took a deep breath and smiled and said, "See, I have been listening."

Neither Jack or Diane believed that they were having a baby; because they decided what they want in life, it just felt like it was part of the adventure that they had decided to start on. It seemed like a nice consequence to their act of deciding.

Jack could hardly believe Diane's total recall.

"Do you have your list of things you want?"

Diane pulled out her notebook and showed him her list. Diane's list was twice as long as Jack's. He started to thumb through it and couldn't believe how detailed every item was she hadn't just written things down: there was the color and the size and how it made her feel. It was like she had a dream about each item and then woke up and wrote all the details.

"I don't understand, I thought you were reluctant to do this? I thought we were setting ourselves up for disappointment?"

Diane put her hand over her tummy: things changed today. Jack looked at her confused.

"The baby!"

"I decided I was going to break the chain of disappointment. I do not want our child to settle for just fine. I want our baby to know early on about the seeds of greatness. I figure I have a good nine months to prove this truth so I can pass it on. I don't want the weeds of disappointment to break him or her as I felt it almost broke us. I believe!"

Jack felt the warmth of love and joy that surrounded Diane. "This is a lot to take in the last 15 minutes." Jack had learned he was going to be a father and that his wife had leapfrogged him in the search and meaning of the first step: knowing what you want. Now tears of joy ran down his face.

✳ ✳ ✳ TRUTH ✳ ✳ ✳

Having a great partner in life can and will make all the difference in your journey. When you have someone who supports you and helps remind you that you can do it, this is the spark that can ignite the fire in you.

The opposite is also true. If your partner constantly tells you that you are no good, that you will never make it, this will hamper your journey to success and happiness. Pick your partner well.

Jack let the joy of the moment fill him. It was a good feeling. It was motivation; he had a new reason to find and test the truth that his boss had been talking about. He would do it. For the first time, he felt a need to prove that the truth of knowing what you want can help you get what you want. He had been inspired by Diane, and he, too, wanted to pass this knowledge on to their child. He got lost in thought for a couple of moments. Diane snapped him back to the now.

"Jack! What were you going to tell me about springtime?"

Jack shook his head as he had to capture his thoughts.

"Yeah, yeah, springtime. The boss said that we all have rich soil and that we have to pay attention to our soil or we will fill it up with weeds."

Diane looked at him quizzically.

"The weeds are the thoughts and feelings that we tell ourselves. They are the self-talk that we have. You will hear people verbalize these thoughts. People say, 'I'm such an idiot. I'm so fat. I'm so ugly. I can't get anything right. I'm a simple person. Nothing ever goes right for me. I'm too old, too young, too fat, I'm not smart enough.' We tell ourselves the half-truths all day every day. They root in our subconscious. It helps us deal with failure and defeat. We allow these terms these words to define us. In some sense, they make us feel better. It makes us feel like we are in the place that we are supposed to be. In some weird sense, it makes us feel comfortable. It gives us an excuse for not stretching and growing. Springtime is where we plant the seeds. It's where we till up the soil and make it ready for the seeds of success, or more plainly stated, the seeds of the things we want. What I have come to realize is that I haven't tilled my soil in a very long time. As I look at my garden, it is filled with self-defeating weeds."

"The unexamined life is not worth living," said Diane. "I believe Socrates wrote this a thousand years ago. Is that what you are talking about?"

Jack barely paused but nodded his head yes.

"For the first time in my life, I understand. I have lived my life like I was on a merry-go-round. I didn't believe that I had any choice in what happened to me. I let every bad experience set itself up in my heart and my mind. I allowed myself to believe I was destined for mediocrity. The sad fact is, I never consciously made this decision; it just happened over time. I became angry when I saw other people become successful. I thought it was unfair. Why should they get all the fun? The whole system seemed unfair. We must level the playing field. Give me what is rightfully mine. I had it all wrong. No one can give you a sense of purpose; no one can give you success and happiness. Yes, you can be given stuff, but it's not quite the same as when you earn it."

Whatever your mind can conceive and believe it can achieve.
—Napoleon Hill

"I have chosen to till my soil. I will do it today." Jack let out a huge sigh.

Diane's eyes were wide, she couldn't believe this had comes out of her husband. "That was a mouthful. Sounds like you've had a lot of soul-searching."

Jack sighed again; his face looked of exhaustion from the work ahead and excitement of what could come. This scared Diane. *Till my soil?* Did this mean dealing with all the past hurt and past disappointment? Were they going to need a counselor? Was she ready to tackle her weeds?

No, even though she was excited for the baby and all the things that Jack was excited for, she wasn't sure where to start tilling the soil.

"I don't have all the answers. But from what I can gather from the stories about the farmer and the boss's own life, we make a decision today that all the past hurts, past failures, and injustices that have happened, we accept them for what they are. We stop letting those things define us. We stop allowing those things to dictate what and where we go in life. We can't change yesterday. All we can do is work on the now. We can't worry about tomorrow because tomorrow may never come. Every day that we wait the harder it is to get started. We must face our fears now."

Jack remembered the story that his grandmother shared with him when he was a little boy and woke up from a nightmare.

"'Jackie, whenever you're scared. That fear looks like a big monster. The monster has a light shining on him from his back. You put that light behind it, it casts a big shadow. It makes this monster looks huge. The farther you run from the monster, the bigger it looks. I want you to be different than everyone else. I want you to be brave and run towards the monster. You see, the closer you get to the monster, the smaller it will get. When you run towards the monster, you get closer to the source, and the source of your fear—i.e. the monster—it is never as big as you see it in your mind.'

"She then took out a lamp and put one of my stuffed toys in a dark room, and turned on the light behind Pooh Bear, we then went out in the hall. She said, 'See how big the shadow looks from here? When we move closer, the shadow doesn't change; but as we get closer, the item that is causing our fear comes into sight, and we can see it's only Pooh Bear. That's not something to be scared of."

Diane was starting to understand. We have a choice to face our weeds. We can decide no matter what has happened to us, no matter the injustices we have the option to not let them rule us. We just need to replace those weeds, with seeds of success and happiness. Diane liked the idea, but bravery was not an adjective she'd ever used for herself. This was going to take some time. Jack was just sitting there marveling at the glow that his wife seems to have now. He loved the look on her face when he could tell she was thinking and contemplating life. He was so glad that he had her as a partner. He decided to not interrupt her and let her just contemplate while he admired her beauty.

After several minutes, Diane came back from that place we all go to when we are in deep thought. She caught Jack looking at her with those loving eyes, and she was reminded why she loved him so much.

"Tell me more. How do we do this? I want to start now."

✳ ✳ ✳ TRUTH ✳ ✳ ✳

Truth without action is wasted. When motivation moves you to decide to do something. You must start now. The decision is not enough. Many people decide to do something, and yet never get off the couch. Start small, and then do that action over and over again. The rule of "compounding interest" will kick in.

"Let me check my notes, I think I wrote down everything." With that, Jack opened his note book and started flipping through the pages. "Oh, I found it." Jack looked up from his notebook. "I tried to write down everything that the farmer told the boss; I will try and fill in any blanks that I missed."

Diane again noticed that he had page after page of the same thing written on them.

"It looks like you wrote the same sentence over and over again."

Jack looked a little embarrassed. It looked like he had OCD.

"I'll get to that; it is one of the actions that we must do to till our soil."

Diane said, "Okay," but she had a look like, *This is where Jack, the boss, and the farmer have all lost their minds.*

"I know it seems crazy, but I promise you, in the short time I've been testing this truth, you're going to be amazed at the results. So, we've talked about the weeds. The negative talk that we tell ourselves all day every day. We need a way to counteract it. It takes self-awareness. We need to be on the lookout for this negative talk. This is going to sound counterproductive, but we need to pay attention to what it's telling us. Too often, we hear the negative self-talk, and we just let it sit there, never really challenging the voices. By not challenging the negative , it is like adding water to the seeds of negativity, and they grow like weeds. We need a way to stop the brain from believing it. We get to decide who and what we are. The boss taught the first truth about stopping the weeds. Every time you hear a negative talk, you stand up and put your arms out like an airplane." Jack got up put out his arms and showed Diane. "Come get up and do it with me."

This is it! The day Jack lost his mind. Diane stood up anyway. How in the world would this help?

Jack could see that Diane wasn't buying it. He knew what she was feeling; he had felt it, too, but he had been doing this exercise for the last couple of days, and it worked.

"Let me explain what we are doing and why. Anthony Robbins taught the farmer this technique. Not personally, but at one of his seminars. The way to stop the negative talk, really the only way to get negative talk to stop is with action. I can't say this enough: We can't will the negative talk away. We can't decide that we're going to stop the negative talk. We can't decide that we're going to start exercising, reading, spend more time with our kids, or procrastinate less. We have to just do it. And I mean to start now, not tomorrow or next week. Every time you hear the weeds sing their song about you, you put out your hands, and you count to three and then you bring them together and say stop."

"Do it now?"

"Yes, you do it now. What can it hurt?"

Jack counted to three, and both he and Diane clapped their hands together and said, "Stop!" They did it three times. Diane was a little skeptical.

"I don't feel any different."

Jack chuckled and asked, "Were you having any negative self-talk?"

"Well, no."

"It only works when the weeds are speaking—or should I say when the weeds are yelling at you."

"Is that what you were doing the other morning in the bathroom?"

Jack smiled and nodded his head yes.

"Does this work?" asked Diane.

"Yes, it seems to work for me. The boss explained, it's like your subconscious tells you one thing, and then your brain jumps to your conscious self. I have no science to back this up. But it feels like the negative talk has become a habit. Like all habits, they just seem to just happen. It's like tying your shoe. When is the last time you thought about how to tie your shoe? When you put on your tennis shoes, you slip them on, and you just tie them. No thought is needed. It happens with our negative thoughts also.

"The difference with negative thoughts is, they don't just happen once. They like to repeat themselves over and over again. When it comes to the weeds, one plus one doesn't equal two. These negative thoughts don't do simple math; They do complicated math. One plus one equals 10 million. They make us believe that our past mistakes equal our future failures, and this just isn't true. We can break this chain of self-defeat. By recognizing when the weeds try to poke their little heads up, that's when we do the 'airplane stop technique.'

"I know it looks weird. But it works. I've been testing it for the last couple of days. It snaps me out of my self-loathing, self-defeating attitude. It reminds me that I may have failed yesterday, but that has no hold on me today."

The affirmation.

"When you recognize that you have weeds in your garden, the farmer said you must pluck them up. I believe that the 'airplane stop' technique is the start. It is the key to plowing the soil. It gets the process started. He also talked about the weeds must be replaced. These weeds must be replaced with the seeds of success and happiness. What I believe he is saying is that we need to reprogram our subconscious minds. We need to replace the negative things that we think are part of our past and part of our present. The mistakes and missteps that we believe define us. We replace these thoughts with who we really can be. The people that we are— the person we want to be."

Diane scrunched up her face. Shook her head and said, "So we lie to ourselves?"

Jack spit out his soda. It went all over the table, and he said, "No, not lie. Tell yourself the real truth."

Diane was struggling with the concept of the real truth.

"I don't get what you mean. How do we know what the real truth is? The real truth is that I am pregnant, I am super excited, super scared, and I wonder if I'm ready for this new challenge. I'm afraid that I will be a horrible mother and a terrible wife. I will teach our baby all the wrong things. What if I'm not a naturally good, loving mom? What if I'm not able to manage all the extra duties? What if I fail at being a mother? I have failed so many times, why will this be any different?"

Jack jumped up again and put his arms out. He counted to three and clapped his hands hard together, and yelled stop. Diane almost fell off the couch. Now she was a little angry.

"Why did you do that?"

Jack smiled and nodded for her to do the same thing.

"This is getting ridiculous…" but Diane stood up and did the clapping thing. "This seems quite repetitive. How many times are you going to do this to me?"

Jack took Diane into his arms.

"As many times as it takes. I'm your partner, I will help you as I hope you will help me stop the weeds. All of those things you just said, are not you. Will you make mistakes? Yes. Will you be a perfect mother? No. But we will focus on what we want to be and have instead of what we might be or might have been. It feels like it's a magnet."

"What do you mean?"

Jack went to the junk drawer and pulled out an old magnet. A bunch of random stuff was sticking to it. He put it on the table.

"How did all that stuff become attached to the magnet?"

Diane looked at the magnet, it had different screws, nuts, and metal shavings all over it. It was disgusting looking. She picked up the magnet and dropped it immediately. The metal shavings had cut her. Nothing severe, but she was bleeding a little. Jack grabbed her hand and kissed it.

"That magnet attracts things by touching them. That's what it does. It draws things to it. It can track good things, like the screws and the nuts, but it can also attract metal shavings by the same token. The metal shavings don't just come to the magnet for no reason. That's not how the laws of our universe work. For the magnet to attract anything, it must intentionally touch it. What it touches becomes attracted to it.

"Our brains work the same way. I wish I knew more about how the brain does it. All I know is the farmer told the boss this is how it works, and it has worked for him. We attract the things that we talk about. We attract the things that we complain about. We attract the things that we hate. Remember the Native American fable about the two wolves? You get the one you feed."

Jack stopped, looked Diane in the eyes, and put his arms around her.

"I'm not sure how I know this to be true. I just know. I used to tell myself over and over again that I would marry you. I believed it with every ounce of my being."

Diane smiled; she remembered the first time she met Jack, she whispered to herself, *I'm going to marry him.* There was still doubt in her mind. She had told herself other things, too, but they didn't happen. Why was this so different? She'd let that sit in her mind for now.

It was almost like Jack could read her mind.

"I know this technique seems way too easy. It looks like it's flawed. We all have hope and wish for something, and it hasn't quite worked out as we wanted it. Maybe we didn't even get close. At least that's what we perceive. I don't think this disproves the law of attraction.

"Think about the passion you have when you get angry and upset. You put all this energy and emotion into talking about the things that you don't want. We reminisce about the injustices that we see, and we send them out like waves attracting those very things, just like a magnet. Those waves touch those negative things and bring them back to us.

"What if we had the same belief, the same energy, and emotion for the things we want? If I put the same emotion and energy into wanting love, financial freedom, friendship, success, and happiness, what are the odds that I will send out the same wave? I believe this success rate goes through the roof. There is plenty of proof out there to prove this theory. We don't see the benefit of this positive practice because we don't get specific enough with the things that we want. We don't allow the waves to touch the specific things that we want. When we are negative, we become very specific.

"When I wanted to marry you. I dreamed about it every day. I imagined what our lives would be like, dreamed about you, and I didn't even know you yet. I knew the type of person you were going to be. When you came into my life, it was like a light bulb went off in my head. I attracted you to me. If we change our thinking and stop focusing on what we don't want, and decide precisely what we do want, amazing things start to happen.

"I think it was the boss who told me about the Sears catalog. Life is like a huge catalog. We just have to pick what we want and then imagine having it. We need not be afraid of the outcome. What if I wish for $1 million, and I only get $10,000, am I disappointed, or am I grateful for the $10,000? For most, they let the disappointment tell them this doesn't work. What if it's a test? What if God is testing us? What if he's saying, 'I know what you want, but I will give you just some of it now and see how grateful you are. Are you worthy of the next portion?' The key ingredient is being grateful."

⋆ ⋆ ⋆ TRUTH ⋆ ⋆ ⋆

Being grateful opens up the universe to receiving more. We can spend our whole lives focusing on what we don't have, which will attract more of not having it. We can focus on what we are thankful for, and we will attract more things to be grateful for.

Diane's heart was starting to soften to the idea. She knew that for too long, she had been a person who complained too much. She had focused more on the problems of life than the things that she should be grateful for. She remembered talking to her boss, and he was always going on about how hard it was to hire good people. He could talk for hours about how nobody wanted work anymore. No one had any work ethic. Nobody wanted a job. This generation was just lazy. He had tried everything to attract people to the business. It was hopeless.

Diane started to wonder, was her boss getting what he had attracted to himself? What if you change what we say, what if we started to believe that hiring good people was easy? Was everyone in the world having a hard time hiring good people? There must be a place where people want to work and make a living. Could she change the signal that was going out? This was a good question. It was a big test though. How could she test this theory. She wanted to test it, but in a smaller way.

Diane shared with Jack about her boss, that he was always ranting about not being able to hire good people.

"I want to change this mentality. But I'm not sure I agree that it will work. How can I test it to make sure?"

Jack was thrilled to test the law in a small way. He, too, had some doubts.

"What if we start with something small that we can attract that shouldn't be too difficult to happen, but still be proof that it works?"

Diane thought for a moment and said, "What if we decide that we are attracting a free cup of coffee every day. It is a small thing with a measurable outcome."

Jack loved the idea.

"This is what we will do. In our journals, we will write, 'I am attracting a free cup of coffee today.'" Diane wrote it down. "Now write it 24 more times."

Diane looked up from her notebook.

"Twenty-four times? Why 24 times?"

"I don't have a real reason for 25 times. It just seems like a good number. When you're done writing it, I want you to imagine how good the coffee will taste and how grateful that it will make you feel. It shouldn't take more than a couple of minutes. I like the 25 times because it makes you concentrate on the free coffee. I feel like, after about the ninth time of writing it, I'll start to believe that I'm attracting the free cup of coffee."

Diane smiled and was willing to try it.

Oops, she giggled to herself. *Not try. Do or do not; there is no try.*

They both sat down for the next 20 minutes, and each wrote out their affirmation statements. *I'm attracting a free cup of coffee today.*

(You do it now—25 times.)

When they were done, Jack went back to the junk drawer, cleaned off the magnet, and placed it on the counter. He then grabbed a couple of Post-It notes. He handed one to Diane, and they both wrote the statement on the Post-It note. When he finished writing the note, Jack took the notes to the bathroom and stuck them on the vanity mirror.

"Every night before we go to bed, you must read the statement out loud 25 times. We can do it while we wash our face and brush our teeth."

Why so many times? This is starting to sound a little tedious, thought Diane.

Jack read her body language.

"We must use the same energy and emotion that we would for the negative thoughts that we send out. We send out our negative thoughts out hundreds at a time; that's why we attract so much crap. We need to send out the good vibrations with the same energy and frequency."

This made sense to Diane. What was the worst thing that could happen? It could waste 20 to 30 minutes or if it worked, she'd get a free cup of coffee. It seemed like a little to do for a whole lot of reward. It was so simple.

If this really works... Hope again started to spring in her.

That night, both Jack and Diane got ready for bed. They each recited their statements that they had written on their Post-It notes. They also wrote it down 25 times.

Jack's Journal

-We must replace the weeds with the things that we want
-Write what you are attracting
25 times at night and in the morning
-Say them 25 times a day
-Use the same energy to attract the good things
-Test it
-Habit stack it-say the affirmations
while doing something you already do. *

FREE COFFEE

The next morning, Jack got up first and made coffee. While he was waiting, he grabbed his notebook and wrote 25 times, *I'm attracting a free cup of coffee today.* When he was done, he gave thanks for the free cup of coffee. He poured Diane a cup and took it to her. She was so grateful for the smell of the sweet aroma of the hot coffee. When Jack held it to her sleeping nose. She yawned and opened her eyes and proclaimed, "It worked! My free cup of coffee!"

Jack laughed and finished getting ready for work.

"It's coming."

Diane grabbed her notebook and wrote the statement 25 times. She smiled as she was writing and could hear Jack reciting the attraction statement while he showered. She laughed to herself about already receiving her first free coffee. She was pretty sure that this didn't count, but she wasn't going to put anything to chance. She made sure that she wrote down in her gratitude statement that she was thankful for the free coffee. Jack left for work, and Diane followed suit. She repeated, "I'm attracting a free cup of coffee," 25 times.

Diane jumped in her car and drove to work. On her way, she decided to stop at Dutch Brothers, her favorite coffee shop. She didn't always indulge in the sweet delight, but she had been talking and writing about coffee, and she really wanted one today. She drove up and placed her order. A large white chocolate latte. If she was going to indulge, she really was going to indulge. As she waited in line, she grabbed her purse and pulled out the $6 that it would cost for her coffee.

When she got up to the window, the nice girl at the counter said, "The coffee is on the house courtesy of the driver in front of you."

Confusion and disbelief covered Diane's whole body.

"You're kidding, right?" Who was it? Did she know the driver? What just happened? Diane gathered herself and smiled. "Can I purchase coffee for the person behind me?"

The girl got a big smile and said, "Of course. That will be $3."

Diane was giggling, she was so happy that she could buy someone a coffee, too. It made this whole experience even better. This was going to be a great day. She gave the girl a nice tip and drove on to work. She took time to be thankful for this little surprise.

✶ ✶ ✶ TRUTH ✶ ✶ ✶

There is enough to go around. But you wanting something does not mean you steal it from someone else. The beauty of this truth is, the more you receive, the more you can give. It multiplies exponentially if you give before you already have. Be a person with a servant heart. By giving, you create energy. You never know what a difference you can make by looking to serve before being served.

75

With every step, Diane gave just a little more thanks. How is this possible? It had to be just a happy coincidence. At this point, she didn't care why it had happened. She was thankful and surprised. She pondered the significance of the free coffee all day.

Jack did not stop for coffee on his way to work. He was the first one in, so he started the coffee for the office. Free coffee seemed like such a small thing to ask for, he pondered the significance of asking, and self-doubt started to creep in. He put out his hands clapped them together and said, "Stop!"

At the same time, Kevin walked in. Kevin let out an expletive that we shall not repeat in this book. But he was quite startled. Kevin looked at Jack and smiled and said, "I see you have been talking with the boss."

Jack, totally unnerved, just nodded his head yes. Kevin was one of the most successful salespeople in his office. He had a knack for talking to people. Everyone seemed to love his wit and his ability to ask questions and then intentionally listen. He made you feel like you were the most important person in the room. Jack liked Kevin; he always seemed willing to give a helping hand.

Jack shook off the embarrassment and said, "Ah, yes, I'm stopping the weeds. I'm stopping the self-doubt."

Kevin nodded.

"The first time I talked with the boss, I swear I was clapping about every five minutes. Stop, stop, stop. It was a bloody circus. It gets a little better the more you practice. My mentorship started with the boss five years ago. At that time, I was the lowest salesperson in the company. I couldn't sell water to a man dying of thirst. I actually started my mentorship with the boss by, well, being a complainer..." (Whiners are wieners.) "I complained all the time. It wasn't fair. The prices were too high, and no one would buy from me. I needed a better territory. This was when I learned the stop technique from the boss. But I'm jumping ahead."

Kevin stopped mid-sentence.

"Hey, the office coffee stinks. It's not a proper cup of coffee. Can I buy you a cup?"

Jack's mouth opened, and nothing came out. It seemed like hours before Jack could get his voice back. So many thoughts, so many *Are you kidding me?*'s and *This can't be happening*'s. No way.

Kevin laughed out loud.

"You must be in springtime."

This snapped Jack back to the real world. All Jack could do was nod slowly: Yes.

"I would love a cup of coffee."

* * * TRUTH * * *

Be willing and ready to accept what you asked for. Rejection is not humility. Rejection is a slap in the face to the giver. The giver receives as much pleasure in giving as you do in receiving. Be open to the gifts that life (God) gives you. Be thankful and remember to pass it on.

Kevin and Jack walked down to the local coffee shop, Costal Coffee Roasters. Jack ordered, and Kevin paid. They found a seat and sat down and enjoyed their proper cup of coffee.

"You said something in the break room about springtime? I'm not sure I caught your meaning."

Kevin stumbled on his words.

"I may have jumped the gun. The boss hasn't told you about springtime?"

"He mentioned it, but what does springtime have to do with saying and writing what I want?"

"Jack, I don't want to ruin any of your time with the boss. Are you sure you want me to share?"

Jack took a drink of his coffee. Kevin was right; the coffee sure was much better than the office coffee.

"I would love for you to share with me what you have learned from the boss. A new perspective would be good for me."

Kevin was already starting to like Jack.

"I will share with you what I have done and what I've learned from the farmer and the boss."

Jack interrupted, "You've met the farmer? I thought he was made up."

Kevin laughed out loud.

"No, he is real and quite wise. He has the wisdom that is quiet and calm. He has eyes that can pierce your soul. And a loving demeanor that melts your heart and your mind. He cares so much for people; you instantly feel that he wants the best in you and for you. I was very lucky to meet him before he passed away. If you met him on the street or at the market, he would radiate love and concern, and you would think he was just a nice old man.

"I guess you really have no idea, the number of people you can touch in a positive way. They had to move his funeral outside into tents because so many people came to make tribute to the farmer. It was amazing the legacy that he left behind; it really was a celebration of life. It was a celebration of people who had taken the truths that the farmer shared and how all these people had put those truths into practice. I was there. They had to kick us out because no one wanted to leave. The stories about the farmer, the stories about the truths that he shared and how those truths helped each person have a better life… The most amazing thing was most of the people shared how the truths were put into practice. It was an honor to be part of the farmer's legacy. It was an honor to continue his legacy, and that's why I wanted to share with you what I learned and what I did to move my life forward.

"I've been in sales most of my life. It can be a very negative field. Think about it. What kind of job gets told 'no' over 70 percent of the time. The only other thing I can think of is the sport of baseball. Batters strike out at least 70 to 80 percent of the time. Hall of Fame batters only get hits a little over 30 percent of the time. That is amazing that a profession that honors players work for only being successful

30 percent of the time. I'll tell you what: when I was in school, I got plenty of 30-percents on tests, and there was no Hall of Fame for me."

Jack nodded his head. He, too, could remember low scores in school.

"It's a different game. These ballplayers know that they won't get hits every time and yet they still come to the plate to take a swing. It reminds me of the quote from Wayne Gretzky:

You miss 100 percent of the shots you don't take.

"When I met the boss, I was having a cold streak. We met for the first time right here in this coffee shop. I was in line, minding my own business, the guy in front of me says to the barista, 'I'd like to buy that guy a cup of coffee.' I looked at him and said, 'Thank you.'

"While we waited, we had time to talk. Small talk at first, but he asked me meaningful questions. It was like he really cared about my life. I told him I was in sales, and he asked me how it was going. I complained that I wasn't on a hot streak, the economy was bad, my product was a little overpriced, and it was really hard to get past the gatekeepers. He then asked me the question that changed my life. 'What do you want? How much do you want to make?'

"I was stunned. Who was this guy? We sat and talked for about 30 minutes. The more he talked and told me about the truths, the more I believed. But it seemed too easy, and it was getting late, and I had to go make some sales calls. He asked me to do two things: One, decide what I wanted, and two, write them down. He told me not to wait until tomorrow but to do it now. He then left. I took the next two hours right then and there in this little coffee shop and wrote out everything that I wanted. It's what the farmer would call the wintertime. I then jumped right into spring.

"I wrote down my 'I am' statements. The statement that I wrote first was, 'I am attracting new business clients every day.' I was tilling the soil. I was replacing the thoughts and statements that were holding me back. I was planting the seeds that would fill the holes that weeds had left behind. I stopped attracting the things that I didn't want. Did the bad stuff stop happening? Of course not. But my mindset changed. I stopped looking at the world like it was out to get me. I stopped believing the world could set my worth. I became a baseball player. Every time I got a 'no' from a potential client, I would go to my car and say, 'Swing and a miss.' I would then proclaim, 'Next batter up!'

"I kept repeating the 'I am' statements. For the next six months, I wrote that 'I am attracting new clients every day.' I wrote it 25 times in the morning, 25 times at night. It became a habit. The results, well, let's just say, they have been phenomenal. For the next six months, I was in a groove, and this name comes up that I recognize, but I'm not sure from where. It was the boss's name. I didn't recognize it until I met him at his office. He remembered me instantly, and he wanted to know if I put the truths to work. I told him that I had and that they had led me back to him. He smiled and we talked for about an hour, and he became a client.

"After we signed the paperwork, he asked me if I might consider working for him. Well, the rest is history.

"It still amazes me how easy the first step in fulfilling your dreams can be. Knowing what you want is the first step. It is so important because without knowing what you want, you can never go to the next season. That two hours I spent writing down what I wanted, I can still see it in all its splendor; it started the process of my life moving forward. I am no longer a slave to how the wind blows. I would let my fleeting wants rule the big picture.

"Before I decided what I wanted, I would let inconsequential things get in the way of what I wanted for long-term. Knowing what you want, planting those seeds in your life actually helps you make better decisions. When you don't have concrete wants, and by concrete, I mean written down goals, you make decisions based on your current obsession. Let me give you a couple examples:

"Before I had my concrete goal of being a great salesperson, I just wanted to be a good salesperson. It was something I just put in the wind. It was a fleeting thought. Something I would say when the bills were due. Unfortunately, that thought wasn't concrete and only had importance when I was in trouble. So even though I said I wanted to be a great salesperson, because it wasn't written down, I made decisions that did not reinforce my goal. The reason my decisions didn't reinforce the goal was because my mind had no idea that I was serious. My mind heard me say lots of things, but nothing that was true to what I wanted. Most likely the reason for the confusion is, I would tell it lots of things that countered the thought that I wanted to be a great salesperson. Thoughts like, *I am going to take off early today, so I can go play video games.* I would have so much emotion and happiness about leaving early... Obviously, my brain believed that this was a better choice and that it was moving me towards my goal for the thing I really wanted.

"When I wrote down my goals, and read them out loud, I moved from winter to spring and started pulling my weeds of self-doubt and self-loathing and replaced it with the seeds of success. Things started to pick up momentum. Don't be fooled. It is work. It can be extremely scary. You will have naysayers the whole way. So many people want to protect you from the pain of failure. They just don't realize that if you are batting 30 percent. You are an All-Star and going into the Hall of Fame. Instead, they focus on the 70-percent strikeouts. When we focus on the wrong things, we will continue getting the wrong results. Make sure you write down your goals. Without this step, nothing else will work. Once you have solidified the goals in writing you move into the spring activities.

"The spring activities, rolled gently into the summer activities. Make sure to ask the boss about the collage of random pictures in his office. When you learn that truth, you will be in the summer aspect of reaching your goals. When I met the boss, I was desperate. I was willing to try anything. I was not in my comfort zone. Always be on the guard for getting too comfortable."

Kevin pulled out his notebook, and on the front page he had inscribed:

The good things in life are the mortal enemy of the great things in life.

Jack like the quote, "Where did it come from? Who said it?"

"Many famous people have said something like this and I'm not sure where it originated from. Voltaire said, "The best is the enemy of the good." Jim Collins, in his book *Good to Great*, said, 'Good is the enemy of great.'

"It reminds me, and I hope it reminds you, that the journey is just as important as the end goal. When we focus on the journey and not just the end goal, we will keep striving for greatness. It's like when you first start exercising; at first, it's a real pain; it hurts, and you don't see why you're doing it. And then things start to change. You start enjoying the pain; or maybe you don't enjoy the pain, but the pain starts to become pleasure, and you start to see the results. You get a little jolt of energy.

"Years ago, I watched a great movie called *Parenthood*. I highly recommend it. Steve Martin is in it, and it was directed by Ron Howard. There's a scene in it were Steve and his wife were arguing about something very disruptive in their lives. In the middle of their argument, Steve's grandmother walks in and just starts telling a story.

"'When I was a little girl, the carnival would come to town. It was amazing, all the rides, the lights, the popcorn and candied apples. There were some people who like the merry-go-round; not me, I like the roller coaster. The anticipation with the climb to the top and then the exhilarating ride to the bottom with all the twists and turns not knowing where you would end up. I could never understand why people would want to just go on the merry-go-round; it only goes round and round. That's not any fun. I will take the roller coaster anytime.'

"Following and doing the action part of this truth's equation will never feel like a merry-go-round. There will be ups and downs, turns and twists, and there will be times that you just want to get off and go ride the merry-go-round. Don't do it! Learn to enjoy the experience, and even though it may be scary and you won't be able to see the next turn, know that the truths that you are learning will not change. We will always attract what we focus on."

Jack and Kevin finished their cups of coffee and headed back to the office. Jack couldn't help but marvel at how this law of attraction worked on the first day. Not only had he gotten a free cup of coffee, he got a deeper look into how the whole process works.

When Jack got back to the office he immediately pulled out his journal and wrote down:

Jack Journal

The things I'm thankful for:
The free cup of coffee.
The opportunity to talk with another believer in the truths.
The acknowledgment that if I do these things,
they will work for me.

4. Write down what you want. It helps you make the right decision

5. 30 percent batting average gets you into the hall of fame

6. Affirmation seem to work

7. You attract what you think about

8. Good is the enemy of Great ✳

DJ (DIANE JR.)

Diane had a good day. The free cup of coffee, well, to be honest was unexpected. There was a part of her that wanted to play it off as coincidence. She kept wondering, *What are the odds of writing down that I was going to get a free cup of coffee today and actually getting one? Did the person behind me also want a free cup of coffee? Had they also had the same affirmation this morning? Does it matter?*

The question of abundance and if asking for something was taking away from someone else was answered. She had passed the free coffee onto the person behind her. In a small way, she felt like she had shared her blessing. Was it possible that her blessing made the person behind her's day a little better? What if that person also decided to share the blessing? How about the person in front of her? Did they know how much the free coffee meant to her?

This felt like the butterfly effect. The thing that puzzled her the most is getting the free cup of coffee wasn't the real gift. The real gift was giving to the driver behind her. This coffee that she shared with a complete stranger seemed more valuable than the free coffee that she had received. She could only imagine how it made the person behind her feel. In a way, this was serving others. She had used her blessing to serve another, and it had made her feel great.

⋆ ⋆ ⋆ TRUTH ⋆ ⋆ ⋆

When we use our blessings to serve others, these blessings multiply exponentially. The truth is, we never know how much a simple blessing shared can change a life. By sharing our blessings, we create a wave of positive energy. If we are willing, we can expand the blessing. We also can stop the blessing dead in its tracks. When we allow the blessing to be expanded, we awaken the lion within us.

Diane let the feeling of gratitude wrap her in warmth the whole day. She felt so good about the affirmation that it felt like she was walking on clouds. Maybe it was the hormones from the baby, but she didn't care. What else had she learned about this affirmation thing? She pondered what Jack had told her. Hadn't he said that she could send out Diane Junior (DJ) when she needed a parking spot? How did he say to use this affirmation? *I don't remember him telling me I had to write it. I think I just need to say it out loud...*

She decided that she was going to do it. She had some errands to run after work. She would put it to the test.

The first stop on her way home was a small butcher shop. It was always a pain to go there because there was never any parking. She wanted to pick up steak for dinner. She was already craving steak and pickles. She just shook her head that she wanted both pickles and steak together. The craving was so strong, she didn't care if she had to wait to find a parking spot. Three blocks from the butcher shop.

Diane said out loud, "DJ, find me a close parking space." She giggled, but she said it again. "Okay DJ find me a close parking space."

As she pulled into the parking lot it didn't look like DJ did her job. Just then she saw, out of the corner of her eye, the backup lights on a red Ford pickup. She stopped and let the truck back up out of the space. She pulled in the space right in front of the door. She turned off her car and looked around with disbelief, she looked around to see how this could have possibly happened. This was impossible. Another coincidence? She couldn't help but smile. She had a little hop in her step.

Okay, one for one. Not enough to decide if it really worked, but wow this could be really cool.

Unfortunately, the butcher didn't have any pickles, so she would have to stop at the grocery store, too. The grocery store was only a couple blocks from the butcher. Diane backed out of the parking spot and headed to the grocery store. As she pulled into the parking lot, she said out loud, "DJ, find me a close parking space."

This time there were no spots on the first pass. Not giving up, she said it again, and made one more pass. As she made the turn a spot was opening up as she pulled in. She couldn't help but giggle and smile. This most certainly was the hormones.

She grabbed the cart and went right into the store to get the pickles. The store was really busy, so she decided to pick up some other things since she was already there. She kept passing the checkout lines, and they were packed. Her cart was full now, and she had gotten a lot more the just pickles. She wondered if DJ could help her at the checkout line. She didn't think about, she said aloud, "DJ, open up a checkup line."

Two people who were standing next to her turned to see who she was talking to. Diane blushed and shrugged her shoulders, embarrassed that she was talking to herself. She just pushed her cart up to the front of the store—wait for it...—and whispered it one more time as she came into view of the checkout stand. She got in line, there were four people in front of her. After waiting two minutes, and yes, two minutes, a new teller opened up a line and asked the person in front of her to come into his line, and he asked her to come, too. All she could do was smile and whisper, "Thank you."

She got back in the car. She had so much to share with Jack that would have to wait until after she prepared the steak and pickles.

Jack will love the steak, and I'm sure he'll think I'm crazy for putting pickles on it. She just smiled and drove home.

Diane got home before Jack and started the barbecue. She knew Jack liked barbecuing the steaks, but she couldn't wait; the pickle and steak combo was speaking to her. She opened up the pickles and ate half the jar before she realized it. If she wasn't careful, she would have to send Jack out for more.

What an amazing day! She kept going over the shared blessing. One kind act followed by another. This is what's wrong with the world. We don't do enough random acts of kindness. She had no idea who was in the front car that bought the free coffee, but she liked to imagine it was someone who was following this truth that Jack's boss had talked about. She had no idea how they knew that she had wished for free cup of coffee. Did they know that it would have the butterfly effect? Why did they do it? Diane did it because she was so moved that she got what she'd asked for, it only made sense that she pass it on. It made her feel so good. She promised herself that, once a week, she would randomly buy a complete stranger a free cup of coffee. If this random free coffee would make someone else feel as good as she felt, she would definitely pass it on. The more she thought about it, the more she realized that giving the coffee to the car behind her was the real reward. There must be a truth here. What was it? She would think about it before she went to sleep; maybe write it down in her journal. She had another pickle.

Jack walked in with the smell of the barbecue outside.

"What we having?"

Diane smiled and said, "Steak and pickles!"

Over dinner, Diane and Jack could hardly finish their meal. Diane actually had no problem finishing her steak and pickles, but she did talk a lot with her mouth full. She didn't care, neither did Jack. The conversation was of pure excitement. Diane shared her story of receiving free coffee from the car in front of her and that she shared a free cup with the car behind her. The amazement she felt by sending out DJ to find her parking spot and how a spot just opened up at the grocery store. Jack's eyes lit up with amazement and awe. He shared his story with his free coffee with Kevin. He was amazed at how he got so much more than a free cup of coffee. The more they talked the more excited they got. It seemed magical.

After dinner, they cleaned the kitchen and sat down on the couch and took out their notebooks.

"It's time we get serious. I'm not sure how much proof we need, but I've decided I'm writing down everything I want this year. I'm going to write it like I have already obtained it."

✶ ✶ ✶ TRUTH ✶ ✶ ✶

Write what you want like you have already obtained them. You are talking to your self-conscience. When you tell your brain what you want, the brain starts the process of making sure you go in the right direction.

Diane nodded in agreement. She was tired now. She told Jack she would start her list tomorrow.

Jack looked up from his notebook, looked her deep in the eyes, smiled, put his arms around her.

"We have put this off our whole lives. This is so important. I know you are tired, but I want us to do the things that successful people do. Successful people do it now. They don't wait. I think it adds power to the activity if we do it even when we are tired and don't feel like it. I don't mean to guilt you into it. It's the small things done repeatedly that will take us to our dreams.

★ ★ ★ TRUTH ★ ★ ★
Successful people do what unsuccessful people are not willing to do.
Don't wish it were easier; wish you were better.
—Jim Rohn

Diane knew that Jack was right so she took out her pen and started to write down what she had been dreaming about. They wrote down everything. It was funny; once Diane got started, she no longer felt tired. It was a bolt of energy that went through her. By the end of the evening, they had their list done.

As they laid in bed, they shared what they wanted with each other. Amazingly, they shared many of the same things. Diane took copies of what they wrote down. She typed them up and put them on the bathroom mirror. It was getting harder to see yourself now, with the affirmation statements and now the goal list on the bathroom mirror. It was odd how seeing the list and affirmations made her feel like they had accomplished something.

Jack came to the bathroom as Diane was admiring her handiwork. He felt good, too.

"The boss says that less than 1 percent of people ever get this far," he told her.

★ ★ ★ TRUTH ★ ★ ★
Knowing what to do and doing it are not the same thing. It takes action.
John Maxwell tells a story that his father used to tell him. John's father use to ask him: "If there are five frogs on a log and three frogs decide to jump off the log. How many frogs are left on the log?"

It's a trick question. There are still five frogs. Deciding that you are going to do something is not the same thing as doing it. Make sure when you decide to do something that you follow the decision with action.

Neither Jack nor Diane knew it at the time, but while coming up with their goals and writing their affirmations, they had finished winter, and they soared through to spring. They were about to hit summertime.

Diane woke up, and she could hear Jack in the shower. She could hear him reciting: "I'm alive, I'm awake, and I feel great." He was saying it with real gusto. It made her smile, and she found herself chanting it, too. She got up and made coffee and gave some to Jack. It'd been a couple months now that they had been working on their affirmations. It wasn't always easy. At times, it was real work. She didn't always feel like doing it. With Jack's help, she pushed through and did it even when she didn't feel like she had the energy or the want to do it.

The boss had been right about so many things. Both her and Jack had become more conscious of how they spent their time. They made a conscious effort to take time to talk. They started walking every morning for 30 minutes. It was one of the best times of the day. It was quiet and calm. They seem to really connect on those mornings. It was like setting up their day for success. It was funny; it helped with the miscommunication that can happen in a relationship sometimes. It was a wonderful habit to be in. He was finishing his last affirmation that was on the Post-It note on the mirror. He kissed her and smiled.

She walked back down to the kitchen, and she was reminded that success is doing the little things every day. No giant leaps needed. The timesheet measurement was great in that it showed Jack and Diane where they were spending their time. The boss had said there are no bad way to spend your time, as long as you know why you're spending it that way. At first, she didn't understand. Watching TV all day wouldn't be the best way to spend your time. She had the opportunity to talk with the boss and his wife about this very subject.

Diane's Journal

–Pickle and steak are great together
–We are not lacking. Abundance is everywhere
–Serve first
–Open your heart and mind to the gifts around you
–Attraction to good things is awesome *

DINNER WITH THE BOSS (SUMMERTIME)

The boss invited Jack and Diane to dinner at their home. Diane was nervous and excited to spend time with the boss and his wife. She had hoped she would be able to ask questions. The boss introduced his wife and called her his "stunning muse."

"Everything I am and everything I will be is because of her support and her belief in me. She believed that I was going to make it, even when I wasn't sure. Having a great partner in life, someone who believes in you, someone who supports you, someone who kicks you in the butt, is one of the greatest assets I've ever had. I'm not sure about everyone, but it has been one of the driving forces in my life. I like to think that I have done the same for her."

The boss's wife blushed and kissed him. She was stunning. She had a natural grace to her. At first, she was quiet, but once Diane got her alone, they talked like they had been friends for years. Diane felt at ease with the boss's wife.

Diane was taken on a tour of the home. The home felt warm and lived in. You could tell this was a place with a lot of love. The boss's wife explained that she had done most of the remodeling herself. It had become a passion. She had made furniture and much of the wall hangings—beautifully engraved statements about love, life, and excelling. There were pictures of all the children on the walls. They still had three children living at home. Diane smiled when she saw the affirmations hanging on the master bathroom mirror. She also noticed an engraved word at the center of the mirror. It said "encourager." She studied it for a moment. It was only that one single word. She liked it, but why was it there?

Noticing that Diane was staring at it, the wife explained the significance of the single word.

"As you probably know, my husband is an avid reader. Every time he finds a book that he likes, and that's all the time, he shares it with me. He loves it when an author quotes another author. It gives him something else to read. Anyway, he was reading a John Maxwell book and John quoted a statement about the power of words. His quote was from the book *Aspire* by Kevin Hall. The quote so inspired him. He promptly purchased the book.

"He got so excited that he kept reading me parts of the book and made me promise to read it, too. I would read it in the morning after he left for work, and he would read his copy in the office. Every night, we would sit in bed and read the parts that we highlighted. He has been saying for years, the words we use have power, but he couldn't really define or prove it. His only proof was from the Bible. Genesis 1:3, "…and God said, 'Let there be light, and there was light.'

"He reasoned if we were made in his image and if God's words were so powerful, maybe our words have power, too. We learned about the word genshai, which means you should never treat another person in a manner that would make them feel small.[6.] We fell in love with that word, a word that we aspire to be. After much discussion, we came up with this word, 'encourager.'

"My husband says that it is what I do for him and the entire family. It's hard to explain, but it gives me focus. In the monotonous times, when I struggle, I can look at that word, and it reminds me of who I am. It snaps me back to my own personal center. He was so happy with the word's origin that he said it was me by definition. The word encourager comes from the old French word 'encoraguier,' meaning makes strong, hearten. Encourage's a verb, too. This was the sealer for me. If you remember back to your English class, a verb is an action word. The key to everything that the farmer taught us is based on action. Knowing that these truths are out there is only the first step. The real magic begins when you put them into practice. All over the house are words of encouragement."

Diane was encouraged by the affirmation statements written on the mirror. She noticed a collage of cut-out pictures on the wall next to the master bedroom. She noticed in the kid's rooms they had collages of pictures also. It was weird. They all looked like a third-grader had cut the pictures out and had randomly pasted them on a board. Each board had different pictures. It was the strangest thing she'd ever seen. She would ask about it after dinner.

After dinner, Diane wanted to ask questions about the time log. The boss was more than happy to discuss the hidden truths as he knew them.

"Jack told me there is no bad way to spend your time. I'm not sure I agree. It seems to me there is a lot of wasted time that happens in my life, and I want to change it."

This time the boss's wife answered, "You are correct. You can definitely waste your time, but that doesn't mean that all leisure time is wasted. What we have found is when we measure our time, we find out what we are doing. We often spent our time doing useless things or fun things that we end up losing time. What I mean by useless, I love going on Facebook and catching up with what my friends are doing, but what we found is that we were spending time right next to each other, but we had our heads buried in our phones. There is nothing wrong with spending time this way, but how much time is too much time? Neither one of us planned on spending an hour buried in our phones. We were appalled after doing the time study. We intended only to jump on and then jump off and do something together. I was only planning on spending 10 minutes; it turned out that the next time I looked up, I had been disengaged for at least an hour."

The boss's wife continued, "Measurement is a key factor. The timesheet that we used to measure how we spend our time wasn't to feel bad. It was to help us see where we spent our time. What was eye-opening is how little time we spent on things that we felt were important. At least the things we told ourselves were important. I don't want to sound like I am preaching, but a time log only works if you first know what you want. It's a way to measure if you are spending time moving toward your goal or away from your goal. It becomes an eye-opening experience when you see where your time goes. When I first started my time log, I wanted to get more fit. We all know the only way to get more fit is to spend time exercising. My time log did not show me spending much, if any, time exercising. It helps to reassess what is important."

The boss chimed in, "I want to have a good relationship with my children and my wife. By using the time log, I was able to see that I was missing out on an opportunity to spend more time with my children. I read somewhere that time equals love. I had spent all my energy on work, and I hadn't saved any for them. This was important to me, so based on my time study, I set a time every day to do something that my children wanted to do. It was important in the beginning to set an actual hard time. I know this sounds odd that I would have to put my children on my schedule. It became one of my wants. I needed to give them the time that they deserved.

"By scheduling a time for each of them, it made me accountable to them, and they would know when we were going to be together. As they grew older, and their time is now their own, they always made sure that they were available for the time we set. It goes back to knowing what you want and writing it down."

The boss took out a piece of paper and wrote:

Wintertime = Decide what you want.
Springtime = Write it down. Create your vision board.
Summertime = Work on the plan. Measure. (The "doing" part.)
Fall = Reap your harvest.

Jack jumped up and said, "Excuse me for a minute while I run to the car." Diane looked at Jack quizzically. "I need to grab our notebooks. I want to write this down." Like a flash, he was out to the car and back with the notebooks. He handed Diane her book, and they wrote down what each season meant.

Diane wrote down wintertime is for deciding what you want, springtime is for writing down and making a vision board. What was a vision board? She wrote that in her notebook, she would ask in just a second. Summertime was for measurement and working the plan. Fall was for the harvest. Diane looked up from her notebook.

"What is the vision board?"

The boss looked at his wife and smiled.

"Honey, you take this one. The farmer taught you about this one."

Jack's Journal

-Time log helps you see where you spend your time
-Is my time spent on the things that are important
-Make time for the important things *

LEARNERS ARE EARNERS

The boss's wife said, "Let me get us some more coffee for this story. Diane, I'll make sure yours is decaf."

Diane smiled. She now had a small baby bump. She touched her tummy and said, "Yes, please."

The boss's wife went into the kitchen and made the coffee, then they went to the living room, and she told them how she learned about the vision board.

"It was many years ago. Let's see…at least 20 years ago. The farmer had invited us to his house one weekend. He said that we, as a couple, needed to be on the same page. He told me that our family goals were like a two-person crew team. We both had to be rowing in the same direction in order to reach our goals. On a two-person crew team, each person had to know where they were going, and then you had to encourage each other along the way. As our family grew, they, too, would need to know how to row. They would need encouragement. They would need to see where they were going. The vision board would do that for us. I asked where he had heard about a vision board?

"The farmer laughed and said, 'I heard about it from Mark Victor Hansen, one of the authors of *Chicken Soup for the Soul*. I was lucky, I happened to go to a seminar that he was speaking at. In fact, I've read every book he's ever written. Many of my philosophies on life stemmed from him and other great authors. If I was honest, none of what I have and will talk about is originally from me. It has all come from great people before me. This whole journey/adventure started after I heard Jim Rome. He asked the crowd if they would like to double their income in the next year. Most everyone put up their hands, but I was the first person to throw my hand in the air. Believe it or not, there were actually people in the audience who didn't put up their hands. Looking back on it now, this saddens me a little: so little belief and faith. It reminds me of the great book *Believe and Achieve* by W. Clement Stone. You must first believe that you can for any of it to work. Sorry I could go on and on about our attitude and beliefs. Jim Rome explained that less than 1 percent of the audience would do what he says. *If you would like to double your income in the next year, this is what you have to do.* He then paused and walked around the stage. *Are you sure you want to double your income?'*

"'The crowd was starting to get restless and yelled *Yes!* The anticipation was growing. He said, *What if I told you it would be easy. Would you believe me?* The crowd got silent, and then it erupted with a *Yes!*

"'*In fact, it's so easy you won't believe me. The problem is that it's easy not to do. This is where most people will get stuck. They can't get out of their own way to do it. They will make excuses. Don't be that person. How many of you want to double your income this year? Now the audience was thrilled and excited and all the hands went up. Okay, here it is. Read 30 minutes a day.'*

"'The air in the room went flat. The auditorium went silent. Jim let it sit there for a minute, he raised his eyebrows and smiled. Obviously, the crowd was confused. He went on to explain, *I'm not talking about reading your favorite novel. You need to read 30 minutes a day in the field that you are in. If you're in sales, read everything you can about how to be a better salesperson. If you're in management, read about how to influence people, read about how to manage your finances, read how to be happy, read about setting goals. Decide today that you were going to learn from some of the greatest people who have ever lived. **Learners are earners.**'*

"'*How do you get started? you might ask. You start by investing in yourself. In the* book The Richest Man in Babylon, *George Clauson writes that the key to success is investing in yourself first. In essence, he writes about living on only 70 percent of what you make. But we will talk about that at a later time. To succeed, you need to invest in yourself first. This is where it gets tricky for some of you. Starting today, get out and purchase your first book. Invest in yourself by reading every day for 30 minutes. Only 1 percent of you will go and get a book today. Of that 1 percent of you who do go out and purchase a book, only 1 percent of you will put the reading truth to the test.*'

"'He further explained go to as many seminars that you can and learn from the people that have written these books in person. Invest in yourself first. The dividends are incredible. I leaned over to my wife and said I can do that. She smiled and nodded her head. That weekend, we started our journey of investing in ourselves. Please write down in your journal the *Richest Man in Babylon*. It is a great first book to read.'"

The boss's wife stopped her story got up from the couch and handed Diane a copy of the book, and said, "This is my gift to you and Jack."

Inside the front cover was a note from the boss and his wife:

> *Jack and Diane, we see great things for you.*
> *Invest in yourself and watch how your life will change.*
> *Sincerely,*
> *The Boss and his Wife*

On the next page was a note written to the boss and his wife from the farmer.

> *Your adventure starts now, do not be afraid. I see greatness in you.*
> *With love and honor,*
> *The Farmer*

Diane's eyes welled up. She hugged the book and put it in her purse. The boss's wife hugged Diane and wiped the tears from her own eyes. The boss's wife cleared her throat and continued the story.

"Enough of that," she said. "The farmer told me that Jim continued and said, 'If you can't afford to buy a book, they have these things that you may have heard of, libraries. They are filled with knowledge, and you can go and check them out. Personally, I like buying my own books so I can highlight the important stuff that I want to remember.'

"The farmer continued, 'Before we left the seminar, I went out into the lobby and bought one of Jim's books. I started my reading that night. Every night at 9:00, I would turn off the TV and read for 30 minutes. I put the law of intentionality to work for me. That weekend the wife and I went down to the local wholesale bookstore. And I bought about 10 books for $50. I read every one of them. Before I started this journey, I wasn't what you would call a great reader. I struggled with reading since I was a kid. It usually takes me twice as long to read as most people. I was diagnosed with an acute case of dyslexia but I did not let that stop me, I learned over time to read faster and faster, and I retained the information.

"'The first year, I read every day, I would highlight the stuff that spoke to me and put it into practice. Not everything worked, but most of it did. Jim Rome was right. I doubled my income in that first year. It is something I still do today. Whenever I feel like I can't figure out what I need to do, I pick up a book, and somehow mysteriously, the answer is found in what I am reading. I always find some nugget of truth that inspires me. *Seek, and you will find,* Christ said this, and I always go to His word first. I can't tell you how many times I have struggled with an issue, and I've just opened up the Bible to a random page, and there is the answer. The proof is in the pudding.

"'The last thing that I remember from that seminar is Jim asked the audience, *What is the one thing that 90 percent of all millionaires have in their homes?* Someone shouted out *Pools!* Another said *Nice cars!* After another couple minutes, Jim stopped and answered the question: *They all have personal libraries.* I knew then that I would have my own personal library. Years later, I learned from John Maxwell that he catalogs every good thing that he reads. I have started to do that also. Now I can quickly find what I'm looking for when a problem arises.'

"The farmer stopped and laughed out loud. 'I've become a storyteller like my grandpa. I get so excited about sharing that I get off track. I'm sorry, what was I talking about?'"

The boss's wife smiled, the boss was like that too when he got so excited about sharing the truth and how to help. He, too, would go off on a tangent. (As a reader of this book, I'm sure you can understand the writer is this way also.)

* * * TRUTH * * *

Reading 30 minutes a day is a great tool for success. Learners are earners. Don't fall into a rut. Expand your horizons. Read about great people. Read about life at a different time in history. Read about trials, defeats, and triumphs. Highlight what speaks to you and catalog it.

Diane's Journal

-Action is the key to the "truth"
-Without action nothing happens
-Learners are earners
-Law of intentionality-set a time and stick to it
-Read 30 minutes a day*

THE VISION BOARD

"'You were telling me about the vision boards.' I reminded him.

"The farmer got up, went into a back room, and brought back a 25-by-25-inch poster board. On it were pictures of various things. They were are all cut out and pasted on the board. There was a new truck, a new couch; in fact, the very couch that they were sitting on. There was a new Dodge pick-up, a picture of the beach, to name just a few.

"'What is this?' The boss's wife asked.

"'They are all the things that we wanted this year. This is our vision board.'

"'I don't understand. Why a vision board?'

"The farmer's eyes lit up like the 4th of July. 'Our brain sees in pictures. Not in words. You've heard the old adage. A picture is worth a thousand words.' The boss's wife nodded her head yes. 'It's the same thing for brains? If I said elephant? What do you see?'

"'I see a big mammal with big ears and a trunk.'

"'Exactly. You see the object in your mind's eye. Did you see the letters that spell the word elephant?'

"'No. I wouldn't even think to do that.'

"'Exactly, even when we want to spell elephant on paper, we first see the creature before we start to write the word. We start in winter, deciding what we want. We then write it down. But to make the process work in overdrive, we must put a picture to it. It's like putting fertilizer in your garden. The pictures help our brains put things in context. This is where the vision board really does its work. What would $1 million look like for you? Are you really wanting to swim in cash? Or is what you want reflected in what the $1 million would do for you. This is the picture that you cut out.'

"The farmer paused. 'Back in the day, every New Year, we would gather the family together and have stacks and stacks of magazines. Each person would go through the magazines and cut out pictures of the things they wanted for that year. We would paste them on the board and hang them in the hall. We would walk by them thousands of times during the year. I would say after the first couple of weeks, we barely knew that they were even there. No one would walk by and focus on them. It was a gentle reminder to our sub-conscious mind that these were the things that we wanted.

"'I can't explain how it works or why it works. I wonder if posting the picture on our subconscious mind keeps us seeing that picture and helps drive us towards it. It might be a light tower in the night to help light the way for ships trying to get into the port. All I know for sure is that our subconscious mind is very powerful. I was skeptical at first, but we had such fun doing it. It was like we made our own Sears Catalog.

"When you do this activity, it moves your life into the next season. The key is that you have to actually do it for it to work. When you have finished your vision board, you then move into summertime, and your brain starts to work on the things you want.' The farmer got up and went to the closet. He pulled out a box and showed me the last 20 years of vision boards that he and his family had made. One of the visions board had a picture of the very house they were sitting in. It was from his first vision board."

The boss's wife got up and left the room. She came back with three boards from many years ago.

"I would like to share a personal story about vision boards and how they work. Is that okay?"

Jack and Diane nodded yes.

"The year we started our first vision board with great success. But I want to share how it worked for our oldest daughter. Our oldest daughter was 10 at the time, and she had a slight interest in horses. Nothing over the top. She just liked them. That Christmas, she had asked for a mechanical horse named Buttercup. It stood about three feet tall, and when you held a plastic carrot to its mouth, its mouth would move back and forth. That's it. This was the only present she really wanted. It cost $389. We were not in the position to spend $389 on a toy that we just knew wouldn't be played with for more than a couple of weeks.

"That year, she didn't get Buttercup. She handled it with grace, but she was disappointed. A week before New Year's, we started collecting magazines for our upcoming vision board. Our daughter got all the horse magazines she could find. To be honest, we thought this was healthy, but we didn't think anything would come of it. Neither one of us knew anything about horses. I'm not sure we even rode one before. She cut out two beautiful horses and put them on her board. Do you know what happened?"

Jack and Diane were sure they knew the answer: "She got a horse!"

The boss's wife shook her head no.

"She did not get a horse. Instead, she got a lot of storybooks about horses, but no horses. The following year, she cut out horses again and put them on the vision board."

"In March of that year," the boss interrupted "I got a call from her at work. She was so excited. I could barely understand what she was saying. She told me that there was a horse rescue close to the house. It was only 30 minutes away; for a 12-year-old, that was close. The horse rescue was designed to teach kids about horses. All she needed was a ride and a signed parent agreement. I told her I would talk with her mother. I thought that it was a good idea. That night, we talked about it and decided we would let her see if this was a pursuit that she really wanted.

"That Saturday, I took her to the rescue. I spent two hours watching my daughter blossom in front of my eyes. This was where she wanted to be. She begged me to leave and come back at 5:00 p.m. I reluctantly went home. I went back to pick her up. She came running out to the car. She made us get out of the car and follow her into the pasture. I have never seen her so animated. We walked in the pasture, and she pointed to three horses.

"'You see the white one, that is Sequoia. He is my horse.' My jaw dropped, and all I could do was make a gasping noise. Thoughts of how could this happen—*I don't want a horse. Where are we gonna put it?* Honestly, I thought I was going to faint. Luckily, she explained, if she worked and volunteered until she was 16, they would train her to ride Sequoia, and he would be hers. My panic subsided. There was no way this 12-year-old would keep this kind of excitement for four years. Oh, how I was wrong! Before we left, she walked over with my phone and took a picture of that horse. We got home. She printed off the picture and put it on our vision board.

"For the next four years, every Saturday, she would make sure we were out of the house by 8:00 a.m. I would drop her off and pick her up at 5:00. I don't think she missed a single Saturday. Every summer, she would go and work at the barn, baling hay, cleaning out stalls, and working with the horses. Every year, she would take a new picture of Sequoia and put it on the vision board. On her sixteenth birthday, the rescue gave her Sequoia. The vision board makes the idea become a reality."

Jack and Diane were awestruck. The boss's wife got out a photo album and showed them the pictures of their daughter receiving the horse. There were pictures of her competing with Sequoia during high school.

For a moment, there was a real energy in the room, like when you open the front door first thing in the morning, and the sunshine covers you with light and warmth. The boss's wife let the moment settle.

"With the vision board, you tell your subconscious mind what you really want. It's like when you tell that little voice to find your parking spot. It just seems to go out and find you that spot. The vision board helps your subconscious do the same thing." ✶

Diane's Journal

–Vision Board–cut out pictures of the things you want
–The pictures settle into your subconscious mind
–It inspires you without you realizing it
–For this truth to work you must do it ✶

SUMMER

It was getting late. Diane was exhausted. The baby was really starting to take her full share of energy. Jack and Diane thanked the boss and his wife for a lovely evening. They drove home in silence, each pondering what they saw and heard. They felt like their heads might explode. So much information, so much hope for the future. A door had been opened for them. It was all so simple.

Diane pulled out her notebook. She wrote in her notebook: *The key to all of it is to know what you want.* She underlined four times. She closed her eyes and took a little nap until they got home.

As they got ready for bed, they each said their affirmations 25 times. Even though Diane was tired, she wrote her affirmations, too. She smiled and thought of the quote successful people do what unsuccessful people are unwilling to do. Then she closed her eyes and felt Jack give her a soft kiss on the cheek and say, good night, I love you. And she was out for the night.

When Diane woke, she couldn't wait to start her vision board. After making coffee, she handed a cup to Jack. They sat in bed and reminisced about the dinner with the boss and the boss's wife. Jack told Diane that while she was taking a house tour, the boss gave them another assignment.

"Another assignment? I thought the vision board was the assignment."

Jack said, "Yes, he's assigned us another also. The boss asked me about our first want. I told him we had decided that we wanted to move into a house. He became so excited. He told me that was one of the first things that he and his wife had decided on also. Remember me telling you about the seasons?"

Diane smirked and said, "Of course, I do. I think about it all the time."

"'In the cycle of life, you have now reached summer,' he told me. 'This is where you put in the work. We touched the summer when you did your time study. With your house, you need to know how much the house you want will cost. Do not get discouraged. It can seem daunting. The truth only works if we put them into action. Let's break it down:

Pick the house you want.
How much is it?
Take a picture of the house and put it on your vision board.
Figure out where you are.

"'The farmer calls this the GPS of life. I will tell you more about that next week. I need you to measure where you are at in comparison to where you want to go? How close are you to your goal? The book that we gave you is a great parable of how to become financially successful. It is one of my all-time favorites. Once you've read it, you will understand the significance.

"'I just realized I'm giving you a total of three assignments. Read *The Richest Man in Babylon* by George Clawson, do the vision board that we will talk about after dinner, and I want you to keep a spending log. The spending log is just like your time log. Everything you spend money on, you will write down—every penny. Write down the date and time, how much you spent, and what you spent it on. If you use your credit card, put that in red ink. Paying for things on credit doesn't seem like you're spending money, but the truth is, credit can kill your dreams. The goal here is to see where you are spending your money. If you are like most people, they have no idea where their money is going. We used this technique to buy our first home. We first decided on a house that we wanted. It seems so far out of our realm, and we almost got defeated before we even started. This will sound weird, but we prayed for wisdom, and it was the next week that the farmer handed me the book *Richest Man in Babylon*.

"'We wrote down everything we spent our money on. It was one of the most eye-opening experiences of my life. At first, it was a real pain. Every time I stopped to get a soda, I would pull out my notebook and write down *Coke $1.25/drink, Hamburger $3.50, French fries $2, gas $75, candy bar $1*... You get the point. My wife did the same thing. Every bill that we had to pay was written down.

"'In the first week, we took our list and typed them up into an Excel spreadsheet. We categorized every expenditure. We did this for one month. Our logs told us a story that had good news and bad news. The good news was we spent a lot of money on nonessential items. We had monthly memberships to things that we never used and had forgotten we even had. It wasn't a lot of money, but it was $10 for one, $5.99 for another. It all ended up to be wasted money. We ate out a lot. We were spending almost $100 a week just going out to eat. The bottom line is, we discovered we had income we could use to apply towards a down payment. We decided that we would sacrifice some things that we really didn't need and use the money to advance ourselves towards our goal of a new house. The bad news is, we wasted a lot of money on nonessential things. These are things that you can't hold or see anymore. By measuring where we spent our money, we could make better decisions, moving forward to our goal. We no longer just bought things without thinking about our goal first.

"'I know I sound like a broken record. This is why knowing what you want is so important. Wanting a house enabled us to take the next step and start making decisions that would take us closer to our goal or further away. Will there be sacrifice? Absolutely. It is completely worth it. Will you stumble? Yes, but now you can pick yourself up and try again.

"'In the first year, we were able to save enough to buy our first home. Track your spending.'"

Jack pulled out a full piece of paper and handed it to Diane. Diane unfolded the piece of paper and on it was a blank spreadsheet with these headings.

Date	Item Purchased	Amount	Category

Diane's Journal

-Vision Board-cut out pictures of the things you want
-The pictures settle into your subconscious mind
-It inspires you without you realizing it
-For this truth to work you must do it *

FORESHADOWING

Diane looked at the spreadsheet. It was starting to make sense. Knowing what you want doesn't mean it will magically appear; it helps you make decisions. She started to see more clearly, like taking one small step would lead to other steps and ultimately to the things you want. It wasn't about right or wrong. It was about making conscious decisions to either move toward your goals or away from them. So many decisions she had made in the past led her in the wrong direction. The problem was, she had no idea she was walking the wrong way. It felt like walking in the dark. You didn't know what you wanted. If you bumped into enough things, you'd just sit down and stop trying.

The idea of recording our spending is so simple. Why have we not done it before?

She took a sip of coffee, and then like a flash, it came to her. The reason that she hadn't thought of it before was because she was focused on the wrong things. She focused on the end of the month. The end of the month is when she looked at the bank account and wondered where all the money had gone. She would complain about not having enough money to pay her bills, not enough to buy a house. It was true they were living paycheck to paycheck. She could hardly wait to see if there was any hidden money. They would finally know about their financial situation for the first time.

Jack was eager to start putting the spending log into action. Jack went downstairs turned on his computer and made the spreadsheet, and printed it off for both he and Diane. Diane made more coffee and watched over Jack's shoulder. She felt good that they were taking steps to reach their goal. For the first time, she felt like they were taking steps in the right direction. She felt a real sense of accomplishment. Jack printed off the sheet for her, and she placed it in her notebook. She was eager to use this new tool. She sat down at the table and started to dream about the home they would buy in the near future.

After a few minutes, she jumped up. Okay, jump isn't the right word. She was very pregnant.

"I want to go house shopping."

Jack looked up from the book that he was reading and said, "Okay, where should we go?"

Diane already knew what part of town she wanted to live in. She told Jack where they were going.

"Is there a particular house that we are going to see?" asked Jack.

Diane smiled.

"No, I just sent out DJ to find us a house for sale."

"Really?"

"Absolutely. Let's go have an adventure!"

Before they left for their adventure, they made sure to write down their affirmations, and off they went.

The neighborhood they were interested in was only 20 minutes away. As they pulled into the neighborhood, Diane said, "DJ, go find us our new home. DJ will find us our new home."

The next 20 minutes, they just drove through the neighborhood, looking at all the beautiful homes. They had done this before, but it was just a dream. This time, it felt more real. Unfortunately, there didn't seem to be many homes for sale. Diane said again, but now with a little more force, "DJ, go find us our new home."

The words had barely came out of her mouth when they came around the corner. A person in a red Cadillac got out of their car and was holding a home for sale sign in their hands.

Jack let out a squeal and said, "Are you kidding me?"

Diane, already knowing the power of DJ, just smiled. Jack turned the car around, and they rolled down the window. The realtor said that the house just went on the market today. Would they like to take a look?

Diane almost knocked the realtor down when she jumped out of the car. Jack marveled at how spry she was for being so pregnant. The house was on a corner lot with a big oak tree in the front yard. It had a huge backyard with plenty of room for kids to play. There was a park right behind the house, so the kids could play on swings and slides and meet other kids. Diane was already falling in love with this house, and she hadn't even seen the inside. Jack liked the three-car garage, and he imagined putting a shop in one of the bays for Diane. He, too, was starting to fall in love with this house.

They toured the whole house and asked if they could take pictures. The realtor said, "Of course." Jack and Diane smiled because they each knew why they wanted to take pictures. This definitely was going to be on their vision board.

They spent a little over an hour going through every room. For the first time, this dream that they had but were afraid to really focus on and work toward seemed real. The vision of living there seemed so real. Diane could see herself in the kitchen, making breakfast and working down in the shop. She could hear the laughter and the love they would share in this home. They decided they'd spent enough time dreaming. Now it was time for reality. Jack found the realtor.

"How much?"

The realtor explained the sellers were a retired couple who had raised their four children in this home and wanted to downsize. They wanted to sell to a young family that would love it as much as they had. She then told Jack and Diane the price. Jack's heart sank, his head dipped, and he thanked the realtor for her time.

The realtor could see the disappointment in Jack's face.

"Are you a first-time buyer?"

Jack nodded. Diane heard the price also. Her reaction was the opposite. She got a huge smile on her face. She started whispering to herself, "We are buying this house this year."

The ride back home was deafening for Jack. Diane kept repeating, "We are going to buy this house this year." She was so focused on her affirmation, she did not notice Jack's anguish. All Jack could think of was how they wouldn't be able to afford it. He didn't make enough money. They had a baby on the way. He could feel Diane's excitement, but they had to be realistic. There was no way they would be able to afford this house.

Tears started to well up in his eyes. He so hated to disappoint his best friend. She deserved so much more than he could offer. He could feel the dread in his chest. It felt like a dark cloud that settled on his mind. He started to get angry. *Why would the boss build us up like this just to see our hopes dashed?*

As he was swimming in his own self-pity, he was brought back to earth.

Diane screamed, "Stop the car, pull over into that parking lot."

Jack almost ran off the road. He was so startled. He looked everywhere; he couldn't understand what was happening. Was there an accident? Had someone run into the road? He looked at Diane, and she was smiling. Jack started to get angry. He had almost peed himself. She was pointing to the park that was just behind the house that they had visited. Jack tried to catch his breath and made sure his heart was able to slow down to a normal rate.

The car barely stopped when Diane jumped out of the car. Jack marveled again at his wife. He couldn't remember a time where she had such a big smile on her face. He unbuckled his seat belt and got out of the car.

"What is going on? You scared the stuffing out of me."

Diane smiled at him and didn't say a word. She put out her hands like an airplane, nodded, put her hands together, and yelled, "Stop!"

Now tears were falling from Jack's eyes. He put out his hands like an airplane and brought them together, and said, "Stop!"

It was quite a scene. It must've looked like two grown adults that had lost their minds. Luckily for them, no one was at the park. Diane put out her arms one more time and walked over to Jack and this time, put them around him.

She brought her lips close to his ear and whispered, stop, and then said, "We will buy this house. I know it." She kissed him on the cheek. "I'm using the law of attraction, and you better get on board. We have work to do."

Jack hugged her tight and said, "I believe."

They hugged for a couple of minutes, and they stared at the house. They stopped for coffee on the way home; no freebies. This time, Jack did buy coffee for the car behind him. Diane's heart swelled with the knowledge that even a simple free cup of coffee could change the course of someone's day.

"I know what we're going to do when we get home..." Jack thought, *Yeah, laundry,* but Diane had other ideas. "We're going to take all these pictures and print them out and place them on our vision board. I'm getting on the Internet, and I am going to find pictures of the furniture that we will put in our new house. We need baby things and everything else. You're going to do the same. We are going to put this into action. We're going to call the finance guy and find out what it will take to buy this house."

Jack was glad Diane was taking the lead on this because, in all honesty, he was scared. He wondered if it was not better just to dream than to know for sure you weren't going to get something. He didn't want to see the disappointment on Diane's face.

It was the weekend, so he wouldn't have to call today. He'd wait until Monday. He would ask the boss about his dilemma. Diane made sure to log the expenses of the three coffees that they purchased. She grabbed her phone and thumbed through the pictures of the house. The whole way home, she talked like the house was already theirs.

By Sunday afternoon, Diane had spent a day and half finding pictures of the things she wanted. She had a picture of the house, a picture of a healthy baby. She had a picture of a body that was pre-pregnancy. She had pictures of healthy food. She had pictures of her favorite vacation spot. She had pictures of all the furniture she wanted for the house. Jack was a little slower at finding pictures that he wanted. He was still stuck in the worry mode. He tried to hide it from Diane, but the worry was just too obvious. Diane knew that Jack was struggling.

"You must have faith," Diane said. Jack shrugged his shoulders. "What do we have to lose? Our whole lives, we have dreamt of things and places. But all they ever were, were dreams. They have been like whispers in the wind. For the first time, we have taken our dreams and solidly planted them in the ground. We have the opportunity to nurture them and help them grow. Even if we fail, won't we be at least a little closer to the outcome that we desire?

"I refuse to be afraid of the outcome anymore. I refuse to live a life that is not a challenge. Reaching for what we want, to reach our goals is only part of the process. Taking chances striving for the things we want by choosing what we need to do. That is how we are going to live. When in doubt, go to work. I will not let fear rule me."

Jack smiled. At least he had a hint of a smile. Diane was right. Sitting and worrying about things did not accomplish anything. He stood up, did the "Stop!" routine, and got to work on finding pictures of things that he wanted. That evening they placed their vision board on the wall right in front of the bedroom door. Diane reasoned they would see it at least twice a day, the first thing they would see in the morning when they woke and the last thing they would look at before they turned off the lights.

Jack had wanted to meet with the boss on Monday, but the boss had to leave town for a week. Jack was disappointed. He wanted to ask him about the fear of knowing where you are on the journey. He was so reluctant to call the finance guy; he was sure he would tell him he was crazy for even thinking about buying a house. Wouldn't knowing take all the wind out of him?

The fear kept gnawing at him. The more he listened, the more certain he was that he was setting himself up for failure.

"Holy crap!" he said out loud. Jack looked around to make sure no one heard him. He thought, *What action can I do to work towards my goal? This thinking is honestly taking me away from what Diane and I want. We want that home.*

Jack grabbed his notebook and added a new affirmation: *We are attracting the funds to buy the house on Palm Way.*

He wrote it 35 times. He would be an overachiever on this one.

Jack's Journal

—Don't let fear get in your way
—Fear = False   Evidence   Appearing   Real
—It's good to have a partner
that will lift you up when you are down
—Make a decision to go for what you want. Jump, correct
course, jump again.
—Believe ✱

MONEY SPENT

Jack and Diane were very diligent about keeping their spending log. Within just a couple of days, they started to see trends. They were not trends that made them happy. It didn't take long to figure out why they were living paycheck to paycheck. They kept spending more than they were making. Somehow somewhere, they decided, even if it was subconsciously, to live like rich people. From the outside, they may look successful, as long as you didn't know where they lived. But on a day-to-day basis, they were pouring out money like they had left the faucet open and walked away from it. They had more automatic withdrawals coming out of their account than they could remember. They were spending about $250 a month on movie channels, music channels, and daily workout apps. It wasn't until Diane and Jack sat down and realized how much money they were spending on things they hadn't even written down on their spending log. It took some detective work by Diane. She would have never found it until she did her spending log. When they started their log, Jack had just been paid. She knew exactly how much was in the account. When they did the first summary, there was less money in the account than she had calculated. When she found the discrepancy, she called Jack into the bedroom.

"Jack, are you sure you wrote down everything you spent money on this week?"

"I was pretty diligent. I may have missed one thing, but I don't think so. I took it very seriously."

Diane was confused. She said, "I logged everything, too."

"What is wrong then?"

"We show an extra $250 out of the bank account."

"That is odd. I wonder if there was some fraud on our account."

Diane grabbed her laptop and logged into the bank account. Everything they had purchased the week was as she expected, not that she liked everything they spent money on, but at least it matched. The last seven items for the week showed automatic withdrawal. She highlighted each item; they all looked like gibberish short-codes for something. None of the charges were outrageous $10 here, $25 there. She totaled up the sum again.

"There was $250 a month of automatic withdrawals. That's a lot of money a month for stuff I'm not sure we even use." After a Google search, she figured out what each expense was for. It was very disheartening. They had monthly automatic deductions for a gym membership that neither of them had used for three years. When Diane calculated the yearly expense, she almost screamed. The other charges were for game service, music, and various movie channels. They canceled everything but one movie channel. They saved $225 on the first try.

Next, she went to work looking at their weekly expenses. It was mind-blowing. They didn't realize how often they ate out. When Jack looked at the dollar amount,

111

he also realized that's probably why he had put a little more weight on in the last year. By their calculations, they were spending about $300 a month on non-tangible things. It was a coffee here, a lunch every other day. Stopping for a snack. An extra-large Coke and some munchies when getting gas. It all added up to buying a bunch of junk that they really didn't need.

"This is starting to explain why we always feel like we are under pressure. We spend our money on a lot of little things. By measuring, we at least know where our money is going."

Diane nodded her head in agreement.

"Without the measurement, we may never have realized that we need to change our spending habits." Diane smiled. "With some sacrifice, I believe we can afford the house that we looked at. We could use the money we are saving for a down payment." She stopped. "You know the money that we aren't spending any more on junk."

Less than a week of measuring where their money was going, they were able to devise a plan. Jack looked at Diane and said, "I believe that the farmer would say we have reached summer; we are plowing the fields."

Diane whispered to herself, "We are buying the house on Palm Street."

Jack heard her whisper and repeated out loud: "We are buying the house on Palm Street!"

Diane said, "Let's go. I want to visit the house."

Jack looked at her.

"Honey, it's getting a little late. I am sure it is not open now."

"I don't care. I want to see it again."

Jack knew it was best not to argue with Diane when she had made up her mind. He grabbed the keys and his coat and said, "Get in the car." ✶

ATTRACTION

It was a beautiful Monday morning. The sun was peeking through the clouds, and the world was coming alive. Jack was already in his office. He had written his affirmations and was about to start his five-minute meditation. A red finch started singing to him through the window. Every morning at 6:45 a.m., the same bird came to his side window and would sing to him for a couple of minutes and then fly off. Same bird at the same time every day.

Jack sat looking out his window. It was close to spring. You could see that things were getting close to budding. It was close to the growth period. There was anticipation in the air. There was a great energy. In nature, plants and animals are not afraid of growth. They welcome it. They anticipate it. He knew spring was not for another five weeks. It felt like that in-between time. That time where you know something is about to happen, but you can't tell if it's good or bad. There was a tension. He was moving out of his comfort zone.

The thoughts and concerns about buying this new home seemed impossible. The chasm seemed too large. Even if you took small steps, it would take forever. His mind wandered to past days of disappointment, missed opportunities and just the days of living in a fog. Lost in a daze and letting fear well up in him, he kept thinking about all the reasons he shouldn't call the finance guy. *Ignorance is bliss,* he thought. It wasn't logical. How could they possibly buy a house? Yes, he'd gotten free coffee three days out of five—lucky coincidence. But a house? He was startled by Kevin, who knocked on his door as he came into the office.

"Hey man, I stopped and picked up some coffee. Do you want some?"

Jack shook his head in disbelief.

"I was just thinking about coffee when you walked in."

"I have actually been here for a couple of minutes. You were in such deep thought, I didn't want to disturb you. I finally made a noise to snap you out of it."

Jack blinked his eyes and felt a little embarrassed.

"What were you in such deep thoughts about? You look like you were in anguish."

Jack took a big swig of coffee, "Diane and I want to buy a house."

"Let me see the picture. You have a picture, right?"

Jack pulled out his phone and showed Kevin the picture of the house.

"That is beautiful. Why the concern on your face?"

Jack shook his head.

"It seems impossible. There are some things I don't know. I am concerned that I will disappoint Diane. What if I can't figure out how to make this work?"

Kevin sat there quietly as Jack seemed to be caught in his own whirlwind of despair. He didn't say anything, just nodded his head. Finally, Kevin did what all great salespeople do. He asked questions.

"What is the worst thing that can happen?"

Jack said, "That's easy. We don't get the house."

"That doesn't really sound that bad to me. On the scale of bad things happening, that seems minor. Is it possible to over-focus on the what if's too much? Sounds like a lot of stinking thinking to me."[7.]

Jack shook his head. He knew that Kevin was right; it just seemed impossible. Kevin stood up, put his hands out, clapped them together, and yelled, "Stop!"

Jack grimaced. He knew the routine. He just didn't want to do it.

"I know, I know I just don't feel like it."

Kevin smiled.

"Yeah, I've been there. Can't see through the clouds. Here's the deal: even on those days when it's cloudy and miserable, there's one constant truth. If you get above the clouds, you will see the sunlight. It doesn't matter how bad the weather is on the ground. The sun is still shining above the clouds. The sun is still there. You just have to break through the clouds.

"Have you ever looked at a bumblebee before?" he asked.

Jack's mind raced, "A bumblebee?" Now he knew for sure that Kevin was pulling things out of thin air. Grumpily, he said, "Yes, I've seen bumblebees before. How is that relevant?"

Kevin smiled at Jack's grumpiness.

"Have you ever wondered how that little bumblebee can fly? It doesn't make any sense. He has this fat little body and small little wings. And yes, even though it's a myth that a bumblebee scientifically shouldn't be able to fly, isn't it amazing? From the looks of it, that the fat little bumblebee should at the very least go on a diet.

"From the outside, it looks like he has no right to fly. If a bumblebee had a conscious mind, I'm sure he would look in the mirror and say, 'Nope, I'm not built to fly. God surely didn't intend for me to fly.' And yet, the very purpose for the bumblebee is to fly from flower to flower. It is his purpose for being here on Earth. Stop thinking that you can't fly—metaphorically speaking, of course. Focus on what can be, not on what won't be. Attract what you want. Even in the darkest days, the sun is still above the clouds.

"I know that it takes energy to fly above the clouds. Action always creates energy. A plane cannot fly above the clouds without moving down the runway. It's full speed ahead and then lifts off. What do you need to do to get out of the clouds?"

Jack shook his head.

"I need to call the finance guy and ask him what we need to do. It is so much easier just to pretend that it can't happen instead of knowing for sure that it will be turned down."

"You are really below the clouds right now. When is your next meeting with the boss?"

"Later today. When he gets back from the airport."

"That is good. Ask him about GPS. Do you have an affirmation for buying the house?"

Jack nodded in embarrassment.

"Yes, I have the affirmation."

"Have you written it down today?"

Jack was starting to feel a little foolish.

"No, not yet."

"Let me see that picture again."

Jack brightened up and took out his wallet, and showed Kevin a folded piece of paper. He gave it to Kevin. Kevin took the picture and let out a little chuckle.

"I know this house. Find me when you're done with the boss—attraction, baby; attraction. Don't forget to move above the clouds. I think you're going to like what I have to share. Write down your affirmations and believe no matter what happens, that house will be yours someday."

Jack felt a little better. He didn't particularly like the "someday" part, but it was nice to have encouraging words.

⋆ ⋆ ⋆ TRUTH ⋆ ⋆ ⋆

When we decide on our goals and believe that they will be attracted to
us, God gives us little clues that we are moving in the right direction.
Be open to the small messages. They are everywhere.
Remember to be thankful.
Don't be surprised, and welcome the message.

Jack's Journal

-The valley is temporary — keep moving
-The Sun is always shining above the clouds
-Action creates energy. Action will get you above the clouds
-Look for the clues that remind you
that you are on the right track
(As I write this a small bumble bee landed on my arm
and hung out for awhile....
interesting may a small clue that this all works)⋆

GPS

"Jack, come in. I'm sorry that we missed last week. I'm so glad to be back. It has been a hectic week. One of those weeks when you feel lost and confused. It felt like I was stuck in the mud the whole time. I'll tell you, it took all the effort I could muster the strength to get out of bed this morning. There were times I just wanted to quit. It's funny how so many things can pile up and make us feel so small."

Jack's mouth was open wide. Thoughts of, *This isn't possible. The boss always has it together. Is he falling apart in front of my eyes?*

The boss raised his eyebrows and took a deep sigh.

"I guess this is a good way to lead us into our next discussion. I believe that you and Diane have done your vision board?" Jack nodded his head yes. "You're doing your spending log too?" Jack again nodded his head. "What have you concluded in the last couple of weeks? Are you measuring your spending?"

Now Jack sighed.

"I'm a little embarrassed. I can't believe how much we have wasted. For years, we've complained that we don't make enough money. The truth of the matter is, well, I do want to make more money, but we spend more than we should on pointless things. We have already canceled things that were automatically coming out of the account. We figured by just canceling all the unused subscriptions, we will save about $250 a month. That was the easy part. Not spending on the things that we don't use seemed like a no-brainer. I decided not to look into how much we have really spent over the last couple of years on things that we haven't used forever. I am not sure I could stomach it."

The boss nodded.

"I know I've been there, too. The difference is, I wanted to know how much I'd spent on useless things as a reminder not ever to go back. I wanted to get really mad. I wanted to make sure I completely felt the pain of my poor decisions. Pain can be a driving force. There are certain decisions that I want to remember, not so I can punish myself. I'm not talking about being a victim; I'm talking about being a victor.

"I want to remember the pain so that I will remember that everything comes at a price. I use my journal as a way to reflect, and it enables me to keep things in perspective. I spent time with the pain with the hope of dissecting it. I asked the ultimate question. Why?

"I wanted to figure out why I made the decisions that I made. What did I get? Was it worth it? Would I do it again, knowing what I know now? What was my trigger? If I could figure out my trigger, maybe I could make better decisions the next time. The farmer called this the GPS of your life."

"GPS of your life? I'm not sure I understand." Jack got his notebook out. He was fiercely writing everything that the boss was talking about. The more the boss talked, the more confused he was getting. "I really need help understanding playing with your pain. This seems dangerous. Don't I run the risk of letting the pain consume me? What is the trick to not letting the pain of my decisions not consume me?"

"I asked the same question. It seems so counterproductive. I'll do you one better: if I focus on my pain, will I attract more pain? That is the exact way I asked the farmer.

"It was one of the rare times that I spent with the farmer. I usually met with the farmer early in the morning. I had been meeting with the farmer for about a year. Things were really picking up. I was practicing all the concepts that the farmer had taught me. I could feel that I was getting closer to the things that I wanted. I was like those marathon runners that could feel the end was near but couldn't see the finish line. I was doing the concepts, and I'd seen and received little gifts that reaffirmed the process, but I had to make some tough decisions, and I was frightened to find out the answers to my questions. When it came down to it, I was afraid of the answers.

"The farmer warned me about spending too much time looking at my pain. He told me that if we are not careful, we can let the pain become sorrow. He told me as long as I looked at my pain like a scientist, and only spend time with it to learn from it."

"You were afraid of the answers?" Jack's heart dropped. He was pretty sure that he understood what the boss was talking about now.

"Yes, I was afraid of the answers. See, I knew that I'd come a long way. I wanted things to happen now. I was afraid if I asked the questions that needed to be answered, I would find that the finish line wasn't as close as I thought it should be. I didn't want to know. It was easier not to know. I had had a day of fear that just seemed to envelop me. I needed to talk with the farmer. I wanted to know, *What now?*

"I drove to the farmer's house on this fairly warm spring evening. The sun was starting to set. Even the warmth of the sun couldn't erase the feeling of dread. As I drove up, I could see the farmer's wife sitting on the front porch, drinking sweet tea. He instantly recognized my car as I drove up. It was like he was expecting me. There was a third glass of sweet tea waiting for me.

"As I got out of the car, he grabbed the glass of tea and brought it to me. By this time, nothing really surprised me about him. But I still asked. 'Were you expecting me?'

"He just shrugged and patted me on the back. We walked to the front porch. I kissed his wife on the cheek, and I took a seat between them. We sat there for what seemed like hours, just listening to the day come to a close. The sound of frogs and crickets filled the air. The sun was setting over his farm, and I started to relax, almost like I was in the dazes. The farmer asked, 'Are you starting to feel better?'

"Oddly, I was. I wasn't ready to admit it or give in, but I really was starting to feel better, so I shrugged my shoulders and gave a half-smile.

"The farmer clapped his hands together. 'Stubborn! Man, I know the feeling.' Without letting me respond, he quoted the Bible. I believe it's Matthew, Chapter 6—'Therefore, I tell you do not worry about your life, what you will eat or drink; or about your body, what you will wear. Is not your life more than food and the body more than clothes? Look at the birds of the air; they do not sow or reap or stow away in barns, and yet your heavenly Father feeds them. Are you not much more valuable than they? Can any one of you, by worrying, add a single hour to your life?'

"He then went very quiet. Almost like on cue, a hummingbird flew next to us and ate from the feeder. I know you won't believe me, but that hummingbird stopped eating and flew right at me, stopped a foot from my face, hovered, and just looked at me. I know hummingbirds can't wink, but I swear he winked at me and then flew away. We sat in silence for a couple more minutes. The scene was surreal. The beauty of nature, the sound of the universe making; well, it lifted the weight from my life, and my worry seemed to be fading. The farmer took a sip of his tea. 'So why do I have the pleasure of having your company this evening?' he asked.

"I took a deep breath. All I could say, and it was barely a whisper, was 'I am weary and tired.'

"I could feel the farmer's wife put her hands on my arm. I looked at her. She smiled. It was warm and understanding. She paused, not taking her eyes from mine, and she said, 'And let us not grow weary of doing good, for in due season we will reap, if we do not give up.' I knew this was a Bible verse, and I had to look it up later. From the book of Galatians 6:9. She stood up, kissed me on the cheek and walked into the house. The farmer just nodded his head in agreement.

"We sat for a couple more minutes in silence. The sun finally completely went down. The silence was filled with the sounds of frogs and crickets. It was a moonless night, and the porch light only allowed you to see so far out in the distance.

"'One of the greatest aspects of living on a farm is how nature can cleanse your soul,' he told me. 'There have been countless nights that I've come out here and let nature do its work…

"'I'll let that sit in for a minute.' Somehow, I knew he was right. Something about being in nature always makes you feel better. Years later, researchers have shown that even a picture of a nature scene can release endorphins in the brain that help relax us. To this day, I'm not sure if the farmer knew about the science; I'm pretty sure he would not have cared. As long as it works, that's all that matters. We sat in silence for a couple more minutes.

"The farmer got up and walked to the end of the porch. He was facing his farmland. He asked, 'What do you see out there?' By now, it was pitch black, the porch light was dim, and you couldn't see more than about two feet beyond the porch. I walked over to where he was standing and tried to see what he was looking at. All I saw was darkness. I would've seen a million stars if I looked up, but looking forward was only darkness. I looked at him, and I looked out again.

"'I don't see anything. It's too dark.'

"The farmer made a grunting noise in agreement. Again, the farmer asked, 'What is out there?'

"'I'm not actually sure other than your farmland,' I replied.

"'How can you be certain?'

"I said, 'The most obvious reason is I'm on your farm. I would guess that you have planted some kind of crops out there.'

"'That would be a good guess. What stage are the crops in? Are they healthy and are they ready for harvest or have they been taken over by weeds?'

"I started to get a little frustrated and said, 'I can't tell from here it's too dark.'

"'But you know that they are out there, right?'

"'I guess I haven't really noticed them until you asked what is there.'

"'Straight in front is corn and to the right is a field of tomatoes. If you take a deep breath, you can smell them. Some are already plump, ripe, and ready to pick. Over there, I have onions. Do you see them now?'

"I look left and right and then straight ahead.

"'No, it's still too dark.'

"The farmer chuckled, 'I guess you're right. Do you believe that they are there? Do you believe me?' He now looked at me and said again, 'Do you believe that they are there?'

"I said yes and then I pointed to the corn, tomatoes, and onions.

"'Good now feel them in your mind. Each plant gives off a different smell, a different sound, different energy. Close your eyes and feel them. I want you to see them as they will look when they are ripe and ready to eat. See the texture; smell their sweetness. Now imagine how they will taste. Now open your eyes.'

"The light was bright. The farmer was holding a flashlight in his left hand, and he was shining on the different areas of the farm. I could see the corn and the tomatoes but not the onions. He then turned off the flashlight. 'Do you know what is out there now? Do you see it more clearly?'

"My mind was racing. The light had helped me see the direction of the corn, and I could see the tomatoes, but it was dark again. It would be easy to forget what was there. My confusion puzzled me. Here he was, standing on a dark, dimly lit porch, looking out at the darkness.

"For a brief moment, I was able to see everything, but then the flashlight was turned off, and now all I had was the memory.

"'I'm not sure that I see it more clearly. What I know for sure is that you were telling me the truth. Each part of your field is exactly what you said was planted there. As far as the clarity of the picture, it is still a little bit hazy. I honestly saw a better picture in my mind of what it will look like at harvest. The light really only showed me where the plants where at in their growth cycle.'

"The farmer nodded in agreement.

"'Imagine that you planted seeds in your garden, and yet you never checked on them. What would you get? How would you know if you had to tend to them?

Each plant requires certain nutrients to continue to grow to their potential. Some may need more water; some need more sunlight, and then others may need fertilization. And finally, some may need to be dug up and replanted.

"'When we start this process of reaching our goals. We need to be able to ask hard questions. We have to work on our system. I call this the GPS of life. I first need to know where I'm going. I have to believe that the place I want to go is really there. I may need to shine a light on it from time to time to reassure myself that I haven't lost sight of it. It is the hardest part for most people to figure out. They become afraid that the work may be too hard and that it's not as close as they anticipated. I need to pull out my GPS and see if I'm getting closer to my goal or have I gone off track.

"Being off track is usually a relief; it allows us to correct our course. The problem is that some goals take longer than others, and when we put our GPS to our goal, we see that we are on the right track, but we still have miles to go. Unfortunately, most people don't want to know. They love that ignorance is bliss.

"'There's comfort in staying in the same place. Never checking the GPS. It gives you a false sense of security. What questions must you ask? If you are feeling pain right now, why? If you don't ever search for the answer, you will become comfortable with the pain and never move out of it. Take for a moment someone who is not physically fit. They feel the pain. They're not sure what it is. They become their own doctor and look up what ails them. They're sure that they can self-diagnose what is causing them pain. This only makes it worse by either believing it's something minor, and they play it off. Or they have a serious disease that is going to kill them in the next three months. In both cases, they stop working on the pain. They fool themselves into thinking they have solved the problem by either not ever dealing with it or worrying about it until it possibly becomes the disease.

"'I believe people are more afraid of knowing the truth than the unknown. You can't be one of those people. When we feel the pain, it's important. The pain is telling us something. We must stop and assess the situation. If I haven't gotten to my goal yet, why? We may have to ask hard questions. I can't plant my garden and then walk away. I need to keep checking on the progress.

"'I need to face the reality of the situation. My corn may not be growing at all. I may be impatient. It could be that my expectations of how fast they should grow are wrong. It may be that I haven't clear knowledge of the maturation that it will take for them to grow. I must ask the question and not be afraid of the answer. By asking these questions, I will have a better understanding of how much further I must go. I will be honest. The answers are not always clear. Sometimes, the only answer you get is that you shouldn't give up. Sometimes all you get is to turn your flashlight and glanced at the end product.

"'Stopping and accessing where you are at in the process, turning on your GPS, should not be a scary thing. It may tell you that you are close to your goal. That could be a relief and add excitement. It may tell you that the road you need to travel is still far ahead. Don't become discouraged. Look back on how far you have come. Be thankful. Your success is not determined by reaching the goal. Your success is determined by how you journeyed. It doesn't end when you reach what you want. That is just the next stepping stone.

"'Focus on the journey. This is working the system. It is better to know where you are in your journey than to be blind to the path. What is the worst answer you can get? Personally, I would rather know where I stand than worry about the unknown. When I don't know and I worry about things that might or might not happen, I cause myself great stress. That stress works us over like a heavyweight boxer taking body shots. The only way we can fix the pain is by knowing what is causing it. Don't let the fear of hard work get your way. When we asked the questions that need to be asked, the journey becomes clearer.'

"The farmer turned on the big floodlights, and I could see all the crops as clear as day."

Jack's Journal

-The valley is temporary - keep moving
-The Sun is always shining above the clouds
-Action creates energy. Action will get you above the clouds
-Look for the clues that remind you
that you are on the right track
(As I write this a small bumble bee landed on my arm and
hung out for awhile....
interesting may a small clue that this all works)*

FACE IT

The boss turned to Jack, "Where are you facing the darkness?"

Jack cleared his throat.

"We found the house we want to buy. I don't know how we'll be able to buy it though. I know when I call the finance guy, he will laugh at me and tell me there's no way I'll be able to afford it. I'm not sure I can handle the disappointment, and frankly, I'm a little angry that I'm feeling this pain."

The boss understood the feeling. He, too, had felt the pain.

Jack explained, "There's a part of me that would rather not face the pain of knowing that it can never happen. It's one thing to think that I can't ever buy the house. It's quite another to be told it won't happen."

The boss sighed.

"Is this the first time someone has told you that you can't do something?"

Jack looked at the boss. His heart was heavy. His whole life seemed like people were telling him he couldn't do things. He had almost until recently stopped trying. In fact, this was the very reason he stopped trying in the past.

"No, I've been told many times that it isn't possible."

The boss waited and watched Jack's head drop.

"What did I tell you? What has been my message to you?"

Jack didn't like this line of questions. He knew exactly what the boss had told him.

"You told me that I could do whatever I put my mind to."

"Please stand up."

The boss put out his arms, and Jack put out his arms and brought his hands together, and yelled "Stop!"

After a couple of minutes, the tension eased. Jack felt a little embarrassed that he kept jumping to the negative chatter. He was thankful that the boss had taken an interest in him.

"It's time for action. What do you need to do next?"

Jack's heart sunk a bit.

"I need to call the finance guy and see if I can get a loan for the house." He pulled out the business card. He handed it to the boss. The boss took the card.

"Let me see the house." Jack pulled out the picture from his jacket. "Well, that is beautiful. I know the neighborhood. Close your eyes and picture right now having a barbecue at your new home. Smell the meat cooking. See all your friends and family there. Feel the love and pride that you have sharing your home. Now open your eyes. We just shined the flashlight on your goal. Now go turn on your GPS. Find out what it is going to take to get there.

"This is the work part of the garden. You are fully in the summer season. This is where the rubber meets the road. We all get lost and weary at times. You may find that your goals are further than you anticipated. You may hear more no's than you ever thought possible. The no's only mean not right now. What have you learned along the way? These are tests, roadblocks, and hurdles that we all must go through. Don't be afraid; it's all part of the adventure.

"The farmer told me, 'We attract the things that we want,' then he patted me on the back and said, 'Take the next step to see where it leads you. I'm going to bed. Stay awhile and enjoy the darkness. Enjoy the sounds of the universe let it speak to you. Then go home and write down all the things that you are grateful for. In the morning, do the thing you are most frightened to do. It's only then that we can make progress.' With that, he walked into the house.

"I sat there for another 10 minutes, taking in the sounds and smells of his property. I pinpointed what I needed to do the next day. And I did it. It wasn't pleasant, but it wasn't nearly as bad as I had built it up to in my brain. The thought, *Do it, do it, do it!* kept echoing in my head. Even today, when I am afraid to ask the questions that I need to ask, I check my GPS.

"Do it, do it, do it," The boss echoed the statement over and over again until he trailed off to a whisper. Jack wrote in bold letters at the top of his journal: **Do it!**

"What do you need to do?"

Jack pointed to the business card.

"I need to call that number and figure out what the next step is on this adventure."

"When will you call him?"

"When I get back to my office." Jack whispered, "Do it, do it, do it!"

"Let me know how I can help. If you don't like this finance person. I have friends that specialize in first-time buyers."

Jack thanked him and walked back to his office. Waiting there for him was Kevin.

"So, how did it go?" he asked.

Jack smiled and said, "Do it, do it."

"One of the best parts of going after what you want is the action part. Not allowing fear to stop you is so refreshing. You know that picture you showed me, of the house."

Jack looked confused.

"Yes, I showed you just about an hour ago."

"Can I see it again?" Jack handed Kevin the picture. "I knew that I recognized it. I know the owner. I grew up with one of their sons. I am glad I was right because I called the parents, and they want to meet you."

Jack blinked several times.

"What do you mean they want to meet?"

Kevin had a gleam in his eyes.

"I told him all about you. I told them about you and Diane. They were thrilled to hear about you. They told me that they wouldn't accept any offers until they met with you. They would like you and Diane to meet them this Friday. They invited my wife and me, too. Say you will come."

Jack's head was swimming. Was this really happening? The seller wanted to meet them? How odd was this? Jack shook his head, trying to grasp what all this meant.

"What time?"

Kevin said that the whole family would be there around 6:00 p.m.

Kevin exclaimed, "What an amazing coincidence!" and walked out of Jack's office. Relief and fear-filled Jack's mind. He was dazed. He opened his journal, and saw written in bold letters: *Do it!*

He pulled out the business card and dialed the number. ✦

FINANCE GUY

On the second ring, a voice answered. She introduced herself as Blake.

"Hello Blake, my name is Jack, and I'm interested in talking about getting a first-time home loan. I have a business card here for Jason."

"It would be my pleasure to help you. Give me a sec, and I will get him on the phone."

Jack's terror was growing. Thoughts of disappointment started to grow. He imagined turning on a flashlight and shining it on the goal. He whispered to himself, "It's better to know where we stand. It's better to know."

After a few minutes, Jason came on the line.

"Hi, this is Jason. I understand you're looking to buy your first home."

Jack cleared his throat.

"Yes, my wife and I are ready."

"I can definitely help with the process. First, let me tell you, we have lots of programs to help you buy your first home. I will walk you through the entire process." Jack started to feel a little at ease. "I'm going to need some basic information, so we can see what lenders will work with us. Have you picked the house yet? And do you know how much they are asking?"

"Yes, we've picked the house, and yes, we know the price."

"Great, we will get to that in a moment. Do you have any questions for me before we start?"

Jack tried to catch his breath. He had more concerns than questions.

"I'm not really sure what to ask. My biggest concern is that you will turn me down. Really, I'm afraid that you will laugh at me and tell me that I am a fool for even asking."

"I completely understand your trepidation. I promise you won't hear that from me or anyone else on my staff. My job is to find you the best deal. I want to make sure that whatever we do makes financial sense for you and your wife. Please understand it may take some work on your part, but we will find the right loan. Having your own home can make all the difference in your life. We pride ourselves on helping people get into the house they want. Rest assured, we will be part of your team."

Jack started to relax.

"What information do you need for me?"

"Let's start with the basic information. Where do you work?" Jack told him. Jason let out and laugh. "I know your business. Did your boss tell you to call me?"

Jack wasn't sure how to answer. The boss had not recommended him.

"No, I am sorry I got your card from the realtor."

"That's okay. I know your boss from college. About 20 years ago, I needed help setting up my business, and he gave me some excellent advice. My fault I have lost touch with him. How is he?"

Jack thought, *Who doesn't the boss know?* and "He is good and busy as ever."

"Now, I'm glad that you called for two reasons. Maybe I can help pay back all the great advice the boss gave me. Okay, enough of that. Let's get down to brass tacts. I'll need your social security number, amount of your salary, and all the pertinent information that a bank would need for a loan. I will pull your credit report and put a plan together for you. From what I have, I feel confident that we will find you a good loan. Let me go to work on this. I will call you tomorrow and give you an update."

Jack started to feel a sense of relief. Maybe knowing where you're at in the process was okay. Maybe knowing the next step would help put his mind at ease. He took out his notebook and wrote down his affirmation about the home on Palm Street.

At 4:58 p.m., Jason called Jack.

"Jack, this is Jason. I have your file altogether. Things look pretty good, but there are a few things that you are going to have to fix."

Jack's heart sank. He could feel the pit in his stomach start to grow. The chatter in his head began to amplify. How would he explain it to Diane? She was so happy. For a couple of minutes, he was lost in his despair.

Jason, sensing that Jack had gotten very quiet, said "Jack—Jack, don't panic." Jack came back from his inner turmoil. "I have seen horrible credit reports before. Yours are okay. We have to tweak a few things, nothing that can't be fixed, I promise you."

Jack was letting the chatter take over. He hardly heard anything that Jason said.

Jason again could sense that he was losing Jack.

"Jack, I know this can be painful. But it doesn't have to turn into sorrow." This seemed to bring Jack back from his chatter.

"I guess I don't understand what you're talking about", Jack said.

"Pain is not bad. Pain is that response that tells us that we need to fix something. It's when we ignore pain that is when we get ourselves into trouble. Or it's when we let pain become something more significant than it really is. That is sorrow. The pain you are feeling now is good; it means we have something to fix, but it is fixable. Don't let this simple pain throw you off track. I promise you, you aren't that far away. I want you to get the best loan, not only for the short term but for the long term."

"What do I need to do? How long will it take to get it done?"

"That depends on you. It could take up to two years or, depending on how much time you spend on it, as little as six months. You could possibly do it in three."

Jack thought, *Six months to two years? There's no way the house will be on the market for six months...*

Jason said he was emailing the things that Jack and Diane would need to do to qualify for the loan. When Jack read the emails, nothing seemed impossible. It was just going to take time. He wasn't sure if time was something that he had on his side. He printed the email and started to prepare himself for discussion with Diane.

Jack said to himself, "Jack, you can do this. Jack, this isn't as bad as you thought. Jack, you are going to buy the house on Palm Street." ✶

RIDE HOME

The drive home seemed to take longer than usual. Maybe that was good. He thought a lot about what Jason had said about pain. Was pain good? He had never thought of it that way. That seemed crazy. Why would anyone seek out pain? Most of the people that he knew did everything to avoid pain. Hadn't he avoided pain at all cost his whole life? The only time he could remember seeking out pain is when he was younger, trying out for the football team. That pain seemed worth it. That pain was physical and it was good. He smiled to himself when he remembered sprinting up the steep hills around his neighborhood. That pain told him he was getting into shape. That must be the good. That must be what Jason was talking about.

But what did he mean by sorrow? This idea was hard to grasp. He now was having a conversation with himself out loud. He pulled over and grabbed Jason's card. Jason had given him his cell number. Jack called. He needed to know more about sorrow.

Jason answered on the first ring.

"Hello, this is Jason."

"Jason, this is Jack, I'm stuck in traffic, and I wondered if you could share with me more about sorrow?"

Jason said, "I'm not an expert or psychologist, but this is what I believe sorrow equates to. Sorrow and/or suffering are when we replay bad events over and over in our heads. For example, you may decide that the conversation that we had earlier today was painful."

Jack interrupted, "It was painful."

"Okay, I will give you that. It wasn't what you wanted to hear, but it is what you needed to hear. And really, there is nothing that I told you that you and Diane can't take care of in a relatively short time."

Jack agreed.

"Let's say you decided on your way home this evening to replay this event in your head. But you decide that our discussion meant the end of your dream of buying a home. You could take our discussion and believe that your pain will be never-ending. You could decide that you are a complete failure and that nothing you do is right. You could use this one painful event to define your whole life."

Jack was stunned.

"Who would do that?"

Jason paused.

"I guess it depends. I think almost everyone at one time or another plays an event that caused them pain and turns it into sorrow. The unfortunate part is that we don't replay the event to improve. We replay the event and things that lead up to the event. We make a single painful event into a Hallmark family movie on why

I am a failure. You have a choice. You can let the pain be a wake-up call, or you call turn it into a life defining moment. Pain lets us know that there is a problem. When we decide that pain is permanent and instead of doing something about the pain, we choose to amplify it by playing it over and over in our minds, this again will lead to sorrow.

"Pain is part of nature. Sorrow is man-made. Pain tells us what we need to work on. Sorrow adds all the pain together and adds it with giant leaps to the equation. Sorrow says if one plus one equals two, then one plus one plus one equals 20. Our emotions get involved, and we start to add pains from our entire life. The truth of the matter is, they only add up in our minds. But in reality, they are merely figments of our perceived truth of the events. I highly recommend the book *Solve for Happy* by Mo Gawdt. He talks quite a bit about pain and sorrow."

Most of the time the only thing wrong with our lives
is the way we think about them.[8.]

Jack was almost home.

"Jason, thank you. I believe I understand. I appreciate your time."

Jason said, "You're welcome, Jack. Do it!" And then Jason said goodbye.

Jack decided he wouldn't let himself panic. He said a little prayer. He thanked God that he had gotten this far. He thought, *Jack, look at the road you have traveled so far. Look at everything you have learned. People you have met, your mindset has changed. Six months ago, you couldn't even dream of buying a home. This is just part of the adventure. I'm attracting a way to buy the house on Palm Street.*

He smiled to himself.

Diane was tracking Jack on her phone. She knew when he pulled into the parking lot. She flew out of the front door and met him before he could get out of the car.

"Did you make the call?"

Jack nodded his head. She hugged him and kissed him deeply. They walked into the apartment.

"Before I let you read the email, you need to know we still have some work to do."

Diane already knew it wouldn't be easy, but she felt up to the challenge. Diane grabbed the piece of paper and started reading. Tears began to leak from her eyes. This was not the response Jack had hoped for.

"Baby, it's going to be all right. We can get this done. We will figure out a way."

Diane looked up from the piece of paper.

"You bet your ass we can do it. That house will be ours."

"What?" Jack was perplexed. She was crying but not because she was disappointed. Jack thought, *I will never understand women.* He kept that to himself. "Why are you crying?"

"Can't you see? We now have an action plan. This tells us precisely what to do. We can do this. There is no doubt it'll be some work, but I love knowing. We have been so frightened of what we didn't know that we let it rule us. I would've been happy even if the road we needed to travel took us 10 years to get there."

Jack's heart swelled, and he thought again, *I will never understand women, but thank God I have this woman as my partner.* He felt waves of love for Diane. This was precisely what he needed. Diane grabbed her notebook and made a to-do list.

"I almost forgot we have been invited to a barbecue Friday evening."

"A barbecue? Where? With whom?"

"Kevin knows the owners of the house on Palm Street. They want to meet us."

"No way!"

"Yes, Kevin told them about us, and they want us to come to visit them and the whole family."

"Isn't that odd? I don't think that's how the process is supposed to work."

"You may be correct, but I said that we would come."

"What do we need to bring?"

Jack looked at Diane with the confused look that men get when wives asked them a question they never in a million years would think to ask.

"I don't know. Are we supposed to take something?"

Diane shook her head. She knew that the joke was trying to figure out what women were thinking, but she was just as confused about how men think. She smiled at Jack.

"I will figure it out."

Jack was relieved.

Jack Journal

—Pain tells us something is wrong
—Sorrow is pain amplified by our emotions.
It is a multiplier of pain
—Sorrow is man made—It serves no purpose.
It is never as bad as we perceive
—It's about mindset
—Setbacks/pain are temporary,
as long as we perceive them correctly *

BBQ

Friday came much faster than expected. Diane was nervous about meeting the family.

This seems so odd. Why would they want to meet us? She had talked to friends, and they had never heard of such a thing. *Maybe they want to judge us, see if we are worthy of their home. What if they think we are the wrong kind of people? Perhaps we aren't good enough.*

Diane shook her head as thoughts of all the reasons why they wouldn't like them came to her consciousness. She let the thoughts surround her and then she stomped her foot and said, "Diane, you stop that right now."

Diane stopped on her way home and bought flowers and an apple pie from her favorite bakery. And yes, she sent out DJ to find her a parking spot. Again, right in front. She was prepped and ready to go.

Jack got home earlier than usual. Diane could tell he was nervous. It all seemed so big. What if they blew it? She just kept whispering to herself that they were going to live in the house at Palm Street. They had nothing to lose.

Kevin told Jack that he and his wife would meet them at the Coastal Coffee Roasters a couple of blocks away from the Palm Street's house. Diane thought, *This adventure is sure ramping up.* She was going to meet all sorts of people today. It sure felt like the roller coaster right now. She was at the peak, looking down at the steep decline. *It's too late to turn back now. We will ride this out.*

Jack was nervous but had a quiet calm about the experience. They had come so far. It was just another small step. He figured this would neither make nor break them.

"I want us to focus on the fellowship. Let's focus on meeting friendly people and sharing love, life, and maybe some wine."

Diane looked at him and said, "No wine for me."

Jack laughed, "Okay, grape juice for you."

Jack and Diane met Kevin and his wife Kelly outside the coffee shop. There was an instant connection between Diane and Kelly. It is a friendship that is still going on today. It was only a short, 10-minute drive to the house on Palm Street. Diane was so excited, she could barely contain herself. She was daydreaming about holding parties like the one they were going to. She knew somehow someway they would live in the house on Palm Street. Diane hoped they weren't the first ones there.

As they pulled up around the corner, she no longer had to worry. The street was littered with cars. How many people were coming to this barbecue? Her heart started to race, and when she saw the house, a relief swept through her. She was ready for the challenge.

Kevin and Kelly led the way. Kevin was right. He seemed to know everyone. There were families from all over the area. Jack wondered how one family could know so many people. They met the owner's grown children and grandchildren. There was a warmth and love that they had never felt before. It made them love the house that much more. They could feel the legacy that the owners had created.

The owner was right next to the barbecue, cooking hamburgers, hot dogs, and chicken. Kevin introduced Jack and Diane. The owner put out his hand shook Jack's hand and gave him half a hug.

"It's my pleasure to meet you." He smiled at Diane and asked permission if he could hug her. She readily agreed. She thought, *What a great greeting!* She wasn't sure, but she thought she heard him say namaste. She looked into his eyes, there was a sparkle, and she knew that is exactly what she had heard. She knew right away that she liked him. The owner said, "Let me find my bride."

He looked through the crowd of friends and family and spotted her playing with one of their grandchildren. He hollered out to her. She looked up, smiled and walked over to them.

"I want to introduce my better half of more than 60 years. I call her Pea because she has been my sweet pea since the day I met her."

She blushed and hugged both Jack and Diane. She asked how far along Diane was, and she took Diane by the hand and led her away to introduce her to the other ladies at the party.

"Is this your first?"

Diane said, "Yes."

"That is so wonderful, exciting, and scary all at the same time. One of the greatest tools in raising my children was having a support system with other mothers. It helped me get through the hard times. Someone to share the experiences with other than just my husband."

They walked over to the picnic table.

"This neighborhood has changed so much in the last couple of years. We are seeing the changing of the guard. I will introduce you to a few of the new neighbors. The first couple just had their first baby two months ago, and the neighbor from across the street, well, let's see, I think she is due in about three months. You know, when we moved here it was the same way; it was a great support. We decided that it was time for the next young family to do the same."

Diane smiled.

The owner's wife introduced her to the first neighbor. She was holding their three-month-old daughter. She was sound asleep in her mother's arms. She looked so beautiful with her tiny pink bow on the top of her head. Diane felt her baby kick, and she thought, *I just met your first friend.* It took everything that she had to hold back the tears.

The neighbor's name was Sydnee. Sydnee gave Diane a small hug. The owner's wife said, "It's a rule in our home everyone is greeted with a hug. Hearts touching hearts."

Sydnee smiled.

"I hear you're going to be our new neighbors. We are so excited that Sonja will have a friend very soon."

Diane's eyes got as big as saucers. She looked at the owner's wife and the owner's wife smiled and gave her a wink. Diane could no longer hold back the tears. They started to leak out.

Diane whispered, "I sure hope so."

The owner's wife led both the ladies over to the neighbor that lived across the street. They walked across the lawn where a very pregnant lady was sitting on a chair. She and Diane could have been twins. Her name was Alivia. Alivia pushed herself out of the chair and made a grunting noise. They all laughed. She touched Diane's belly and said, "You must be close."

Diane nodded, "Just a little over three months left."

There was an instant connection. They hugged the best they could. Alivia and Sydnee were terrific. Alivia asked, "So when are you moving in? I see that they took the for sale sign down."

"I'm sorry, they did what?"

The owner's wife had walked off to greet other guests.

"Oh yeah, they took the sign down on Monday. They told us they were selling it to a lovely young couple with a baby on the way. They were so excited to share with us the news. They told us that it was just a dream come true. Our three homes have quite a legacy. It seems that the couples that owned our homes became lifelong friends with them. If you look over by the fence, that gentleman in the baseball cap, he and his wife sold us our home. That's his wife with their daughter and three grandchildren. Over on the deck is the other family that sold Sydnee and her husband their home. It was more of an interview process than a sale of the house. It was weird in a way. It was like we were led here."

Diane was perplexed and bewildered. The dazed look was unmistakable and she felt a little lightheaded.

"What's going on? What you mean you were led here?"

Both Sydnee and Alivia looked at each other and said, "The boss started us on this adventure."

"The boss? How do you know the boss?"

Alivia chimed in, "I have never met him, but my husband hasn't been able to stop talking about him. They met about three years ago at a conference. My husband was just drawn to him. They were standing next to each other in line to get into the conference, and the boss asked my husband what he was hoping to find at the conference. That conversation revealed that my husband hadn't decided what he wanted from the conference.

"From there, we learned about the truth of knowing what you want. My husband started meeting with the boss once a month. and we began to put the 'truths' to the test. No, try; just do."

All three ladies started to laugh.

Sydnee said that she and her husband met the boss and his wife at church.

"They took a genuine interest in us. They have been the catalyst for our transformation as well. Our lives have become an adventure. We met Alivia and her husband a year ago after we moved in. They have become one of our best friends.

"Do you have a move-in date yet?" asked Alivia.

Diane looked down at the ground.

"This is the first I have heard that we bought this house. We haven't even made an offer. We just found out there are some things we need to do to qualify for a loan. There is still some doubt that we will be able to buy."

Sydnee squeezed Diane's arm.

"We went through the same thing. We were sure that it would take too long to get all the finance stuff in order. It took us over a year, but the family that we bought the house from waited for us."

"These old neighbors had a plan. They knew what they wanted for the new owners of their homes. They had a vision and we fit their vision. I am sure you have heard of the farmer."

Diane's eyes lit up.

"Yes, the boss tells Jack about him all the time."

"These three neighbors were friends with the farmer. They have been using the farmer's truths for ages. It's amazing the legacy that knowing what you want and believing that there's an abundance that can be shared with others can create."

Diane could feel the tears collect in her eyes. She knew that she already loved these people and that this was where she and Jack belonged. She hoped that Jack liked the husbands as much as she loved the wives. She looked for Jack, but he was nowhere to be found.

Kevin grabbed Jack a beer and introduced him to the new neighbors. Calvin was married to Sydnee. He owned a couple of pizza places around town, and Tim was a teacher and coach. Sometimes you have an instant rapport, and this was one of those times. It helped that Kevin initiated the conversation by explaining that they, too, worked with the boss. Each shared how they had met the boss and where they were at in their journey. They had so much in common. For just a minute, Jack was caught up in his thoughts. He was reflecting on his vision board. He had cut out pictures of friends on his board. It looked like they were at the party.

Calvin told Jack about his pizza business and how he had the vision to open another store. Jack and Kevin marveled at Calvin's success, and they were impressed by how Tim was using the same techniques to teach the next generation. It felt like these three men had known each other since childhood.

Jack was awestruck by the experience. Could this really be happening? Did the vision board really work like this? It was hard to argue with what was going on right in front of his eyes. ✦

THE STUDY

The owner of the home found Jack and asked if he could have a moment with him. At this point, Jack had no idea that he and his wife had already announced that they were selling their home to them. This, in fact, was a housewarming party for them. The owner walked Jack into the study. It had a warm feel to it; bookcases made out of mahogany. The owner noticed Jack admiring them.

"My wife made them. She got tired of all my books lying around the house."

"Did you read all these books?" asked Jack. "There must be over 3,000 books."

The owner smiled.

"I reckon I have. There are more in the garage. I guess I've been curious all my life. I think you could say it's my escape. I love testing what great people say and do. One of the greatest lessons I have learned is that the trials in life aren't a bad thing. I think they are from God. What makes you stronger? The path of least resistance or the way that stretches your mind, heart, and soul? Is it possible that we are given challenges not to punish us but humble us and help us grow? When we have the right mindset, we realize that those challenges shape us and make us stronger. As my mother used to say, it builds character."

Jack smiled. He hated that saying, only because it was so true. Hard to accept when you're going through the trial.

"Jack, my wife, and I want to sell you and Diane our home. We have taken it off the market. We believe that you are the owners we have attracted to our home. We have been looking for you for almost a year now. When Kevin called and told us about you, we knew this house should be yours. We invited you over here to make sure you are the right fit. My wife has already given the okay. She has absolutely fallen in love with Diane. She even heard her whispered that this was going to be her house soon. I think it made her tear up a little."

The owner grabbed a tissue and wiped his eyes. Jack wasn't sure what to think. In his mind, he kept looking around to make sure that the owner was talking to him.

Jack whispered, "How? Why?"

The owner smiled at him.

"I wish I could give you the answer to how it all works. All I know is when we decide what we want and put it out to the universe, we start to attract it. We pull it towards us when we stop worrying about the how and trust in the Almighty things begin to come our way. At the very least, it helps me make decisions and go in the direction I want to go. When we stop focusing on all the reason something can't be and start focusing on what life can be, life's challenges seem a little better. Have you talked with the finance guy?"

Jack's head was spinning. All he could do was nod his head yes.

"Excellent. After dinner, we want to sit down with you and Diane and devise a plan. Is that okay?"

Jack's mind was racing. What was happening? Is this how all home sales go through? No. The pressure… What if they couldn't get everything done that Jason wanted them to do? They couldn't let these kind people down.

The owner could see that Jack was in shock.

"Jack, stop. Don't worry. There is no pressure. If you want this to be a blessing, it can be, or you can see it as a curse. How you determine to look at it is up to you. Blessings are all around us. The blessing is that we found the family who will carry on the tradition of a loving home, where there will be love, laughter, and warmth. We believe that these blessings are all around us. We just have to stop and listen."

With that the owner smiled, patted Jack on the shoulder, and said, "I better get back to the barbecue. Kevin will probably be burning those dogs."

Jack followed the owner out to the backyard. Kevin was indeed burning the dogs. Kevin could see through the smoke that Jack was in shock. Kevin grabbed Jack by the shoulder and led him to the front of the house.

"What did you do?" Jack asked.

Kevin feigned a look of I have no idea what you're talking about. A sly smile came across Kevin's face.

"I didn't do anything other than help out some friends. The boss had a little to do with it also."

"Why would you do that? What do you have to gain? I don't mean to be ungrateful. How about the struggle? How do we grow without the struggle?"

Kevin was patient and listened as Jack aired all of his concerns and worries. After Jack finally took a breath, Kevin asked, "Do you feel better?"

"No, not really."

"All I did is talk with the boss. We both know the sellers. We called and talked to them about you and Diane. That's all we did. They took the ball and ran with it. Sometimes things work out that way. You haven't been given the house. You have the opportunity now. That's all anyone can ask. You and Diane have to do the hard work.

"This is part of the beauty of knowing what you want. People show up along the way to help. It happened for me, it happened for the boss, and it happened for the owners. It's all about abundance. It's like Ralph Waldo Emerson said:

It is one of the most beautiful compensations in life.
We can never help another person without helping ourselves.

"We are charged with sharing our abundance. Just remember this as you move forward. Now, find Diane, stop worrying, and celebrate your blessings."

Jack was still in disbelief. He said, "You are right. I am sorry. I lost my mind for a second. This is a great blessing."

Jack and Kevin walked back to the backyard and caught up with the group. The neighbors surrounded Diane. She was genuinely enjoying the new friendships. They were laughing and enjoying each other's company. Jack kissed Diane on the cheek. After a few minutes, Jack led Diane away from the group. They walked to the front of the house.

Jack tried to stay calm, but his fight or flight process was in full tilt. He walked Diane to the corner of the yard. He didn't want to seem obvious that he was freaking out. He had that crazed look in his eyes.

Diane knew precisely what was going on.

"I'm guessing someone told you that they were selling the house to us. Don't panic. That's just neighborhood gossip."

Jack shook his head no.

Diane squinted her eyes and asked, "What do you mean no?"

Jack took a deep breath. He felt like doubling over.

"The owner called me into his study. They want to talk to us after dinner. They want to sell us their home. They have taken it off the market."

Diane let out a squeal of delight. She felt the baby kick. Now she needed a deep breath.

"This whole party is for us!" Now Diane shook her head. "For us?"

"Yes, for us a sort of housewarming party."

There was no panic. Diane looked back deep into his eyes. Jack felt like she was penetrating his soul.

"I told you we were going to buy this house. Don't worry. We will meet the challenge."

Jack was still in disbelief, but he knew Diane was correct.

"The timing is right. We can get done everything that needs to be done. Now that we know what it is. As scary as it was to find out how far we still have to go, at least we know. And finally, we can see the light at the end of the tunnel. This is a blessing."

Diane's eyes were glimmering from the sun. She was aglow. Jack marveled at his wife. He thanked God in his mind right then and there that she had said yes. Diane's excitement couldn't be contained. It was like a light bulb went off in her head.

"I've had an 'aha moment.' We worry too much about the *how* we will get to where we want to go; that's not for us to worry about. We need to focus on the *where*. 'How it will, works itself out and is none of our business,' or at least that's what Steve Harvey says."

"When we plant the seed and then nurture them, they will grow. She let out a little giggle, and hugged Jack, and said, "No worries. Let's enjoy the party. Let's meet and enjoy our new neighbors." Jack squeezed her tight. For which Diane said, "Too tight, now I have to pee."

They laughed and went to find the bathroom. ✶